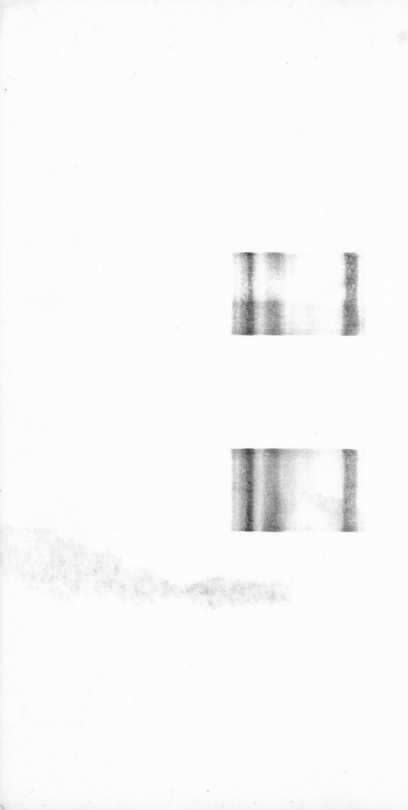

The Treasure of the

White Army

THE TREASURE OF THE
WHITE ARMY

by Nicholas Svidine

Translated from the French by
Leonard Mayhew

Hart-Davis, MacGibbon   London

Granada Publishing Limited
Published in Great Britain 1976 by Hart-Davis, MacGibbon Ltd
Frogmore, St Albans, Hertfordshire AL2 2NF and
3 Upper James Street, London W1R 4BP

ISBN 0 246 10795 2

Printed in Great Britain by
Fletcher & Son Ltd, Norwich

*To the memory of my brother, Ivan, who was killed at
eighteen years of age in Russia during the Civil War while
serving in the ranks of General Wrangel's army*

Publisher's Note

This unusual story of high adventure was discovered by Robert Laffont, the well-known French publisher, who responded to a mysterious note which read as follows: "I have an extraordinary tale to tell. But I cannot reveal my identity unless you are interested in its publication. I am, in effect, the keeper of a number of secrets. Place an ad in France-Soir. Indicate the hour when I can telephone you and meet you personally. The ad should read as follows: Robert Laffont asks Nicholas to telephone him on ————— day, ————— hour." The result is Nicholas Svidine's dramatic account of the legendary White Army treasure, which has been acclaimed by the French press.

Preface

The story of my odyssey with the "treasure of the White Army" will bring down criticism on me from every side. My Russian fellow exiles will be incredulous. Many others will say that I had no right to keep the existence of this fortune a secret. They will tell me that others had a right to know about it. But the truth is that I didn't know whom to tell. And I sincerely believed that no one had a better right to the "treasure" than I.

Actually, however, in the end the "treasure" and my many attempts to recover it ruined my life and brought me nothing but terrible moral and physical anguish. I risked my life for it. Others died for it. If it had not been for the treasure I could have led a normal life — done normal work and earned normal satisfactions.

It's too late for regrets, but enough is enough, and I am forgetting about the treasure. It will never be found, because I could never possibly describe where it is and how to find it. After so many years even the landscape must have changed considerably. No, I am the only one who might be able to identify the place, but I shall never go back to Bulgaria to try.

I will be condemned as well for having sold secret information to several governments. But the fact is that these countries struck good bargains — whatever they may say now. And it kept them on their toes. Even the Soviets have no complaint; most of my "information" came from their weekly, the *New Times*, which at that time had a small foreign circulation. I shall explain why and how I became an "informer" for the United States and for Nationalist China.

I know only too well the risks involved in publishing this story, because I have already suffered the most cruel punishment — exile.

I

Officer of the Czar

1

Siberian Spring

NOVEMBER 1920. The steamship *Vladimir* was docked at Theodosia, on the Black Sea, the decks, cabins and hold all filled with Cossack soldiers. There was no room to budge. From the city came the constant sound of gunfire and bombs. To prevent the Reds from getting our stores we had set fire to warehouses that were filled with all the things we had lacked so sorely at the front: uniforms sent by the English, canned food, everything we had needed. Thousands of riderless horses galloped in confusion all over the beach while their Cossack masters wept at having to abandon these comrades who had saved their lives so often. Those of us on board were anguished at the sight of the English cannons that had arrived just too late to help us. The soldier-workers and the Greens — Bolshevik partisans who operated in the forests and mountains — wanted to block our escape but were afraid to advance on us even now. Defeated by superior numbers, ironically, our departure was a kind of victory: our enemy's bitterest defeat was its powerlessness to keep us from getting away. The last Cossacks mounted the gangplank, their rough faces twisted with confusion and despair. None of us had ever been outside Russia. Now we were leaving forever.

Eventually, I found a warm place to sit, propped myself up against the smokestack, and looked back over my short life. I was twenty-two. I had grown up on a small estate in the Cossack territory of Kuban. My family had lived for generations in the Caucasus, a land with rich resources, pleasant climate and natural beauty. But when Russia conquered the Caucasus my grandfather had decided to settle on the Kuban.

All the men in my family had been soldiers. No other way of life had ever occurred to them. My great-grandfather had fought the fierce Cherkess, a people of ancient Islamic culture who were unbelievably fanatical and fiercely courageous — and armed by the Turks. And the men in my family were giants — my relatives considered it tragic that I had stopped growing at six feet. Only half jokingly, my father and grandfather had dubbed me a freak. My father was a strict but scrupulously fair man whose rewards and punishments were always deserved. He was six feet six inches tall. My mother adored me but she interfered between us only when she thought my father had gone too far in finding fault with me. Since family custom dictated that I be "toughened up," I was sent at eight years of age to a boarding school a hundred and twenty miles away. I hated it at first, and would cry myself to sleep each night. But I got used to being away from home except for vacations.

When world war broke out in 1914, I was a teenager, the kind of student who did just enough to get by. My father had died two years before from wounds he had received in the Russo-Japanese War. When war came, my whole upbringing had led me quite naturally to dream of gallant exploits. I was disgusted with myself that I was too young to join, but the war ground on and by the end of 1915 I was seventeen, old enough to volunteer. I had set my heart on becoming an officer.

The army had lost so many that an accelerated officer training course had been established — four months instead of the usual two or three years; you could complete your course work after the war if you lived that long. I was still technically a year too young to be eligible for the military academy, but it was now possible, because of the circumstances, to take the examination whenever one felt ready. I didn't tell my mother, but I began to try to cram a year's work into the shortest possible time, and I often studied until the early hours of the morning. After three months, I notified the director of the school that I was prepared to take the entrance examination for the military academy. Because of my mediocre school record, he thought I was just mouthing off. But I persisted, and he finally gave in, warning me that no special allowances would be made and that he was all but certain I would fail. But I passed the difficult examination with flying colors, much to his surprise.

"All those years you've been pulling the wool over our eyes," he said, "pretending to be a second-rate student."

"I want to go to war so much, it has worked a miracle," I told him.

I had not given my mother even a hint of what I was up to because I knew she would object. And of course when I showed her my report card and told her I wanted to enter the military academy, she was vehemently opposed and refused her consent. Since I was a minor, I could not join without it. But a month of arguments, pleading and tears finally won her permission, and on a day that was glorious for me and sad for her, I donned my uniform and set off for the reserve battalion stationed at Ekaterinodar, the capital of the Cossack Kuban territory. I had requested assignment and been given to a military academy that had just been established at Tashkent in central Asia, a region I had read much about in school, so, carrying my free railway ticket and all my documents, I said good-bye to my mother and family and set out on the long trip.

Anyone who has not experienced the immensity of Russia firsthand cannot grasp what a voyage lay ahead. It was freezing cold and the train was so packed that I counted myself lucky to find a tiny space in the baggage compartment. Even the corridors were crowded with soldiers on their way to and from the front. Near Tzarizin (later Stalingrad) a snowstorm nearly buried the train, and it took two days of going hungry and nearly freezing to dig ourselves out. The returning soldiers were frantic at the thought of losing precious time from their short leaves. All the way to Samara (Kubichev) on the Volga the train inched slowly forward between mountains of snow.

On the other side of the frozen Volga, I changed trains

for Tashkent. Now, even the third-class cabins were almost empty. The countryside was a constant surprise to me. The Russian forests had given way to desert plains where only small bushes, called saksaule, could grow. Whenever the train stopped, the nomadic Kirghiz rode up on their ponies to stare at the demon locomotive; the railroad was new in central Asia, and the people of the steppes would ride hundreds of miles to see it.

At last we reached Tashkent. We discovered we were only part of a steady stream of Cossacks arriving from the Don, Kuban and Terek territories. The director of the military academy was overwhelmed by us all, and put us on a railroad car and off we went to Irkutsk in central Siberia.

I found Siberia even more dramatic than central Asia. Even though it is intensely cold in western and central Siberia, there are seldom any strong winds, and so it is not unpleasant. The air was so still that the smoke from the engine rose straight up into the air; there was not the slightest breeze. The most extraordinary thing, though, was the overwhelming, absolute silence that fell whenever the train stopped. It was haunting. Occasionally the quiet was broken by a piercing sound like the crack of a gunshot, as a tree would explode in the thirty-below-zero cold.

The military school at Irkutsk consisted of a long, one-story building with a huge courtyard in front and riding grounds behind. It had been established in 1872 to train officers for the crack Siberian divisions. We were welcomed by the director, who declared us officially student-officers, *junkers*.

We had four months to be transformed into officers.

Into those four months, we had to cram what would take two years in peacetime — classes, drills, riding. We were up at 6 A.M. and retired at 10 P.M., with only two hours in between to ourselves. Each night I threw myself exhausted onto my bed, wondering whether I could stand the intellectual and physical punishment. But in a month's time my young body had become so hardened that I no longer felt the least fatigue.

Spring in Siberia is the most beautiful I have seen anywhere. It happens suddenly as the bright sun melts the last traces of snow. We used to take map training on the other side of the majestic Angera River, and from there we could see a breathtaking woods, all white birch surrounded by the freshest, greenest grass in the world. Once I gave in to the temptation to stretch out on the grass — but I leaped to my feet the second I touched ground: underneath the green grass, the earth is eternally frozen. On a day in May, a few days before the end of our course, we took a train to Lake Baikal, about thirty-eight miles from Irkutsk. It is the deepest lake in the world; the water is like crystal and the banks are a scene out of a fairy tale. It was warm so I put on my bathing suit and dived in. To my shock, the water was so cold I felt as if I were being boiled.

And then we were commissioned as sublieutenants. Foreigners could not possibly understand what that meant to us. In czarist Russia an officer was received everywhere, and admired and respected by everyone. He had to wear his uniform at all times in public, and no one, especially women, could resist him. And there were many courtesies. For instance, at the theater, officers never remained in their seats during intermission. Even the Czar observed the formality.

By custom, the entire school was turned over to the new graduates on the eve of graduation. The officers all stayed away and the school orchestra played only for us. Legend has it that the famous poet Lermontov, who had been a *junker*, had designed the ceremony we observed. We danced and sang the whole night long and in the morning we took our time getting dressed since there were no officers to make us hurry. We put on our new officers' uniforms, still with our cadet insignia on the epaulets. By 9 A.M., we were assembled in the courtyard. The authorities arrived with the governor-general of eastern Siberia at their head. For the last time we listened to the command "Come to attention!" as the director read the telegram from St. Petersburg that said that we were commissioned. Then we broke ranks and dashed to the dormitories to take off our cadet insignia. Back in the ranks, we were greeted as "my fellow officers," and then we all filed past the officers, who shook our hands and congratulated us. We thought it unbearably moving that the customs were observed even though we were "twelve-day wonders."

After the ceremony, we were each issued twenty-five rubles. Many of my older comrades went to one of the numerous geisha houses, but I had decided to have dinner in a good restaurant, and I had a date with a pretty young Siberian girl I had met on leave. Then I took her to a concert by the famous singer Plevitskaya, who had sung before the Czar. Two days later, our arrangements were made, and we started on the long trip back. I was sad to leave my girl, and the marvels of Siberia, but I had a month's furlough and I longed to see my family and home.

2

First Feat of Arms

I WAS APPOINTED to the renowned 22nd Plastonais battalion — of the Cossack infantry. We were deep in the mountains on the Caucasus front, and life was very hard. There were almost no paved roads, which was particularly hard on the injured who had to be moved to hospitals, since everything had to be moved by mule. We were always short of provisions, and when food did arrive, it stank so much we had to force ourselves to eat it. There was no firewood in those cold, barren hills. And at night, hungry jackals prowled close to our tents. War wasn't the game I had dreamed about as a boy; suffering attacked before the enemy.

When our battalion moved to the front lines I heard for the first time the sounds of bullets whistling by me. Like us, the Turkish artillery had only small mountain cannons but the cannonballs made a terrible noise as they echoed over the cliffs and through the gorges. I soon learned, however, that there was more danger from rifle bullets, either hitting directly or ricocheting off the rocks. The first day on the front lines three of our men were killed and several wounded.

Our commanding officers planned a major offensive. Because one of our lieutenants had been seriously wounded, I was assigned to direct the reconnaissance operation. October 4, 1916 — I remember the day clearly. I set out at nightfall with twenty Cossacks. My orders were to push forward about two miles to a demolished Turkish village. The night was very dark and windy. I divided the men in two, one group under my command and the other led by a sergeant who was infinitely more experienced than I.

If the first detachment were ambushed, the other was to counterattack from the rear. We wrapped our boots in cloth to dull the noise of our heels on the roads. As we got near the village, we came upon a man sitting on the ground. One of our soldiers jumped him and pinned him to the ground, holding his Cossack dagger to his throat. I heard him say the word *kardash* ("friend"); he was unarmed. One of the soldiers who spoke Turkish soon found out that he was an Armenian, and that his family had been killed by Turkish soldiers. Only he had escaped. He had been hiding in a cave for several days, was without food, and was now trying to find the Russian troops. He told us there were more than fifty soldiers and two officers in the village and that they had at least two machine guns. I decided to dare it. I signaled the other group that they were to attack from the left as we came in from the right. The Turkish position was directly in front of us.

Our battalion was called the *plastounis* (from *plast*, the

word for bed) because they were famous for surprising
their foes at night by crawling up on them on their bellies.
This is the way we moved now. It took us an hour to
advance another half mile, but we surprised the Turks
and took them in twenty minutes. We captured one officer
and nineteen troops, and lost four killed and seven
wounded. From a distance of two and a half miles the
main Turkish force opened an artillery barrage, but the
Russian artillery returned their fire to protect our retreat
and we got safely back with the Armenian, our prisoners,
the two machine guns, and documents that would prove
useful. For my first feat of arms I was promoted to lieutenant and received the order of St. Anne, which is worn
on the saber and bears the inscription "for courage."

That Christmas on the front was the saddest of our
lives. Cold and hungry, all we could think about was the
gaiety and beauty of the traditional Russian Christmas
celebration. (We had no way of knowing that this would
be the last Christmas of the Russian Empire.) During
January and February the cold was so intense we could
not undertake any serious action. But we knew that spring
would bring a major campaign designed to knock Turkey
out of the war.

News from Russia arrived a week late, and we were
stupefied when we learned that a revolution had broken
out in St. Petersburg, and that the Czar had abdicated in
March 1917. I had been raised with a deep devotion for
the monarchy, and these events seemed to me unbelievable, even catastrophic. The ordinary Cossacks were as
broken up as we officers. None of us could imagine living

without the Czar. The Cossacks had always been the main protectors of the throne, and they wondered what their fate would be in a republic and feared that the revolutionaries would never forgive their support of the Czar.

The Russian infantrymen on our right had received the news with boisterous joy; we could hear them cheering in their camp. Ten days later they sent a delegation to find out how the Cossacks, whom they disliked anyhow, would react to revolution. They were astonished and angered to discover that strict discipline still prevailed among our troops — none of us would wear the red ribbons that decorated their coats. We begged them to go away and leave us alone, but that infuriated them further and led to threats against us. After that our general ordered the Cossacks on a double alert — against the Turks and against our fellow troops.

A few days later, the famous order NI of the new government arrived, abolishing all discipline in the army. All military formations, large or small, were to be governed by committees elected by the soldiers. The committees were to be in charge of everything, even military operations. The rejoicing of the ordinary soldiers can be easily imagined; they hated their officers. Many of the officers of the regular army were severely harassed, and some were even arrested for their harsh treatment of the men. The Russian soldiers were furious when they found that the Cossack committees were ninety percent officers (as opposed to only three percent — mostly young revolutionary officers — among the regulars).

When the soldiers learned that the new government

was promising to give them confiscated land, they had only one idea — to get home before the distribution was completed. They deserted the front en masse. The Cossack formations, however, maintained discipline, closing their ears to propaganda. But by November 1917 our presence on the front was no longer of any use. The Cossacks started to return to their *stanitzas* (villages, or administrative districts).

At every railroad station along the route, soldiers ordered the Cossacks to turn over their officers, and the Cossacks, with machine guns mounted on the trains, would reply, "Come and get them." Thousands of officers were assassinated during these days, but not a single Cossack officer was touched.

During a stopover at Prochladnaya, I put over my uniform an overcoat that had been lent me by a friend who was the battalion physician. I didn't think my officer's gold braid could be seen, or that the tiny gold crown on my fur hat would betray me.

"Look, comrades," a soldier called out, "There's an officer disguised as a soldier."

A crowd gathered around me and I was forced to remove my coat. On my uniform were my lieutenant's epaulets. The soldiers seized me and began to carry me to their camp behind the station. I was sure I was going to be torn to bits.

Two Cossacks who did not even belong to my battalion saw what was happening to me and dashed to their trains yelling, "Quick! The soldiers are going to kill a Cossack officer."

About a hundred Cossacks grabbed their rifles and chased away the soldiers, who were beating me as they dragged me along. The Cossacks charged after them with bayonets. My would-be executioners left behind one dead man and ten seriously wounded. Some from my battalion carried me to the officers' car, where my doctor friend gave me a big glass of vodka. "Those bastards did a job on you but there is nothing serious." I was covered with bruises and both my eyes were so blackened I could barely see.

Our train started up again. A division famous for its revolutionary ardor was waiting at the Goulkevitchi station. Whenever a train arrived they would ask if there were any officers aboard. They would drag their unfortunate victims out of the cars and murder them with unbelievable cruelty. As we pulled in, we saw some soldiers but they simply stared at us with hatred. The stationmaster told us that they had got wind of the incident at Prochladnaya and had decided to let us be.

Our regiment arrived finally at Tichoretzkaya, a major railroad junction where everybody was given leave but me. Our commander, Lieutenant Colonel Postovsky (who was to play an important role in my life), did not want my mother to see me in the condition I was in. It was hard to be so close to home and not to be able to see my family after such a long absence. Even more, the thought of being seen in such a state by one very special person with blond curls and wonderful blue eyes was worse.

Ten days later my face was almost back to normal, and the cuts and bruises could be passed off as signs of valiant deeds. But as I was packing my few belongings to go home, the colonel summoned me.

"You cannot go on leave. The commander-in-chief of the Cossack divisions has ordered me to send an officer to Baku on the Caspian with a confidential dispatch. You are the only officer I have that I trust. I'm sending you."

"But Colonel, I shall never return. You saw what the soldiers did to me."

"I know it's dangerous, but it would be for any officer. I have had word that most of the soldiers have left the railroad stations. It's less risky now. You will take the Rostov-Baku express, which has an armed guard under an officer."

I was given no choice. I was handed a large sum of money and documents asking the authorities (but what authorities?) to assure my safe passage. I went to Ticho-retzkaya, where I caught the train for Baku. It took two days. In Baku I bought my mother and brother Christmas presents — a case of the local mandarin oranges. I also came down with a fierce sore throat and a fever.

Just before I was to leave for home, our train was over-run by soldiers who were fleeing the front. Compartments that were intended for four people had to accommodate eight, and even the corridors were packed. I wore an en-listed man's coat over my officer's uniform. I was prostrate on an upper berth and obviously sick as a dog. Thinking I was one of them, the soldiers kept asking me what was the matter. I pointed to my throat and whispered a few words in an indistinct, hoarse voice, conscious that my accent might give me away.

My fever rose and, off and on, I lost consciousness and sank into delirium. I was blinded by my own sweat, and from the overheated, crowded compartment.

One of the soldiers said to me, "Comrade, you should take off your overcoat. It's hot in here and you are burning up. We will just lay it over you." Some of the others rose to help him. I was too sick to care. When they took my coat off and saw my insignia, there was a disquieting silence. Then someone said, "There must be a medic on the train. Someone should ask in the other cars." A very young soldier replied, "You're right, comrade. I'll try."

Soon he was back with a medic, who swabbed my throat with some awful-tasting medicine. It worked like a miracle and, by morning, I was a lot better. He came back later and gave me some more medicine, and by evening I was almost myself again.

I was astounded and very moved by the way these soldiers treated me. They were always solicitous, asking me how I was, and whether I needed anything. At each stop they would fetch boiling water to make tea. All during the three-day trip these companions looked after me, and when I arrived at Tichoretzkaya the whole car came out to shake my hand and wish me a safe trip home. A little while before soldiers had tried to kill me. Now other soldiers were doing all they could for me, with great kindness.

When I reached the *stanitza*, I delivered my report to the colonel as well as the receipt for the package. He complimented me for a job well done, had the treasurer advance me three months' pay and gave me a paper for an unlimited leave. I would never return to my battalion. It no longer existed.

Leave papers in hand, I set out for home and my mother, who was overjoyed to see me all in one piece. It was two days before Christmas 1917. I forgot about the dire political situation, the Bolsheviks, the threat of civil war, and the soldiers on the trains looking for officers to kill and I thought only about my joy in being home at last.

The next day my mother told me that my close friend, Lieutenant Joukov, had been killed just a few days before. He had survived the war, his own men worshiped him, and he had been assassinated by soldiers from his own country. I was beside myself. I dreamed of rallying the Cossacks of my *stanitza* to revenge the Cossacks.

In fact, the czarist government had always had an incredibly foolish relationship with the Cossacks. They were the protectors of the throne, the bodyguards of the Czar and his family, and yet they had always been looked on with distrust. It was a policy that was based on the memory of the revolts of the Zaporov Cossacks — now only about half of those who lived in Kuban — under Stenka Rajin and Emilian Pougatchev, both Don Cossacks. Pougatchev had threatened the reign of Catherine II. The government had then adopted the policy of colonizing the Kuban Cossack territory with Russian peasants, who were encouraged to buy land on low-interest loans from a specially constituted bank.

The intricate social organization of the Kuban Cossacks endured in spite of all this. To rid herself of the troublesome Zaporov Cossacks, who lived in the southern Ukraine, Catherine II had moved them to the rich lands of Kuban, which had been conquered from the Turks, along the banks of the Kuban River, one of the swiftest and most dangerous in the world. With this act, the government both neutralized the Cossacks militarily and consolidated its new frontiers.

When a Cossack reached sixteen, he received from the government a piece of land called a *nadel*. The parcel varied in size depending on how much reserve the *stanitza* held, but it was generally thirty or forty acres. Every four years the land was redistributed, a system that impoverished the famous black soil. As the Cossack population increased, the *nadels* became smaller and smaller and the Cossacks, especially those who lived along the Caucasus frontier, grew steadily poorer. They, the masters, became poorer than the Russian peasants who had been thrust into their midst.

The government was not really giving the Cossacks much of a gift when it ceded land to them. As soon as he receive his *nadel*, at sixteen, the Cossack began his military service, though he remained in his *stanitza* until he was twenty-one, and only then left to join his regiment. A special instructor oversaw his military education. By nineteen, he had to have all his own equipment — uniform, boots, linens, saber and dagger, and a horse if he served in the cavalry. Each year his equipment was inspected. The government supplied only a carbine to the cavalrymen and a rifle to the infantrymen. Equipment was an enormous outlay for these men, who had then to serve actively for five years, and then remain at the disposition of the State as reservists.

While he remained in the *stanitza*, the young Cossack did not merely undergo intense military training; he also continued his regular schooling with a tutor. By the time he joined his regiment, he was a first-class soldier. Since the officers were usually Cossacks, the discipline in the regiments was a family affair. Courts-martial were very rare, and only convoked for the most serious offenses.

Life in the *stanitza* was based on a strict code of honor. In my own I never heard of a divorce, a theft or of any dishonesty. Money was loaned and borrowed on a man's word.

The Cossacks very rarely intermarried with the Russians in their midst. They were very pious, and their own marriage ceremony was extraordinary. The Orthodox rite is very solemn and beautiful, but among the Cossacks it achieved a singular romanticism. The groom, in his full dress *chercheska*, would gallop through the village with his closest friends, all firing their pistols into the air, to meet his bride. She came out to meet him with her attendants and was escorted to the church by the groom and his companions. After the religious ceremony the feast would begin at the bridegroom's house. The dowry — furniture, linens, maybe even oxen harnessed to a wagon — was exhibited for all to see. Late in the evening the newlyweds were led to their room by the *svacha*, the matchmaker. The next morning she triumphantly exhibited the sheets as proof that the bride had been a virgin. The feasting lasted three days.

The czarist government did not trust the Cossacks. The *ataman*, their administrative chief, was always a Russian, just as the Czar's bodyguard was always commanded by Russians or German-Russians.

The Civil War proved how fatal this policy had been for the Czar, and how unfounded the mistrust had been. When the Bolsheviks took power, the transplanted Russians joined them and fought the Cossacks who joined the White Army. (Later Stalin declared the Russian peasants *kulaks* and they lost everything.)

3

First Reverses

MY MOTHER WAS VERY WORRIED about me, and urged me to go for a while to Ekaterinodar, where she thought I would be safer from the Russians. She was not afraid for herself or my younger brother, because she was on good terms with the Russian peasants. To please her, I went, but I found the city in turmoil. The garrisons of Ekaterinodar were filled with soldiers who had, for a number of reasons, stayed behind instead of returning home. It was almost as if they had received some mysterious order to await events. The famous General Kornilov had arrived in the Don Cossack territory and was fighting the Bolsheviks. He was a remarkable man. During the war he had commanded the famous Iron Division. Wounded and captured by the Austrians in the Carpathians, he had escaped, crossed Austria, and reached Russia. He was commanding a corps-on the front when the Revolution broke out.

At first, he was on good terms with Kerensky, who

named him commander-in-chief, but relations between them quickly cooled. Kornilov schemed to be rid of Kerensky, and thereby had him arrested and imprisoned in the small city of Bichorv. With the help of his personal guard he escaped and reached the Don.

On my arrival in Ekaterinodar I saw a notice in the regional newspaper from a Colonel Galaev inviting officers to join a detachment he had formed to keep order in the city. His small troop was temporarily lodged in the empty junior seminary near the railroad station. I presented myself to the colonel, who made a strong impression on me. He received me graciously and informed me that I would serve as a simple soldier like all the others in the detachment. I would have to remove my officer's epaulets but he made me head of the machine gun section, which was my specialty. I had two heavy Maxim machine guns and two light Colts. Besides sidearms we also received regulation Russian army rifles. The date of my enlistment, January 9, 1918, was the day that determined the rest of my life.

Another detachment similar to our own was under the command of Captain Pokrovsky, who held the Cross of St. George, awarded only for the highest acts of heroism. Pokrovsky impressed me even more than Galaev. He was a medium-sized man with an unforgettable face. His hawk-like eyes both attracted and disturbed me. They were cold and ice-gray, and seemed to reach into one's soul. His movements were violent and brusque; his voice imperious even with his superiors. An unusual man, he had so impressed the *ataman* of the Kuban Cossacks that he had

made him commander-in-chief of the troops in Ekaterinodar, and then colonel and general in quick succession,
though he was not a Cossack.

Our two detachments were to disarm the soldiers who
spent their time at Bolshevik propaganda meetings. We
put their arms, including their cannons, into trains. As a
reinforcement for my section, I received two young fe-
male first lieutenants. They had been students at the time
of the Revolution and had taken advantage of the rights
granted women by the provisional government to take
accelerated officer training in Moscow. They were named
Barkache and Zubakina, both very pretty girls. They demanded that they be treated as any other officers, and
once we had all got used to this, we got on very well. And
they were very brave, as I was to learn a few days later.

Toward the end of January, my section was ordered
to accompany some officers from another section to
Ekaterinodar to inspect trainloads of merchandise. We
had received a report that the Bolsheviks at Novorossisk,
the great Black Sea port that they held, had sent arms and
ammunition to fight against General Kornilov at Rostov-
on-the-Don.

I left the women officers in the barracks and ordered
them to clean and grease the machine guns. At the station
we searched the trains and found nothing. As we waited
on the platform for the rest of the detachment, which was
working on the other side of the tracks, a very long train,
loaded with merchandise from Novorossisk, pulled in. It
was crowded with soldiers returning from the Turkish
front. They recognized us as officers.

"Look, comrades! They are not satisfied with having drunk our blood for centuries. Now they aim their guns at us and our brothers."

The heckling led to more serious insults and threats. The situation was becoming dangerous. We couldn't abandon the comrades we were waiting for. The senior lieutenant, Roschin, ordered me to go for the machine guns, and the others to take cover in a small brick building at the end of the platform.

I ran out of the station and jumped into a carriage. I had to pull my gun to persuade the driver but a few minutes later I was at the seminary.

Barkache and Zubakina helped me load the two heavy machine guns onto the wagon. As we approached the station I heard bullets whistling. The soldiers were firing on the small brick building. Russian stations do not have gates, so we would have to try to drive the wagon right up to the platforms where the long train was stopped. I ordered Zubakina to shoot at the cars. With the other machine gun I opened fire on the soldiers who were shooting at our comrades from the platforms. The soldiers began to jump onto the train, or tried to take cover under the cars. The engineer, a Red, saw that things were going badly and pulled the train out.

Another five minutes and we would have been lost. They would have torn us apart. There were many wounded and dead on the tracks, and we telephoned the hospitals to send people to care for them. The episode had serious consequences; it unleashed civil war along the Kuban. As it turned out, the Reds had been getting ready to attack; we found an attack plan on the body of a Red officer.

Within a few hours our intelligence informed us that the Novorossisk Bolsheviks were organizing a punitive expedition. Trains loaded with armed soldiers were on their way to Ekaterinodar and would arrive at night. We were in great danger, since we were at most two thousand fighting men, all officers. Ataman Filimonov held a council of war. Colonel Galaev was to defend the city along the railroad track. Pokrovsky was to set out under cover of dark and attack the Reds from the rear. I would put my machine guns near the railroad bridge and defend the track and the paved road, the only access to the city, which was surrounded on all other sides by an impassable river marsh.

I placed a heavy machine gun on each side of the bridge. The women sublieutenants, protected by steel shields mounted on their guns, fired in bursts as the Reds opened fire on our position, which was only about fifteen yards wide. I fired from the bridge with the light Colt, also protected by a shield.

I had never heard so many bullets whistling around my head. Thousands of soldiers were aiming their fire at our small position. The women showed extraordinary courage and coolness. I was afraid they were taking too many risks by standing up over their shields and I yelled to Barkache to get down. But she stood up for a fraction of a second to turn the gun around and add water to cool it, and in that instant was shot in the heart. A short time later Colonel Galaev was killed in the same way.

Finally, when Pokrovsky arrived and attacked from the rear, the Reds fled with heavy losses, abandoning their weapons and the trains. But our victory was saddened by the death of Barkache and our commander. In the evening we brought their bodies to the seminary to prepare them for burial. As the funeral procession passed through the city on the way to the cemetery, the whole population lined the route.

Captain Pokrovsky was made colonel and commander-in-chief of the entire garrison. The fighting continued to rage. The Reds were furious at their rout and were determined to take revenge. Replacements joined them from every direction and we were sorely pressed, particularly since eighty percent of the population were partisans of the Reds.

Civil war is the ultimate horror. I was in a battalion that was directed against my own *stanitza*. When I heard the cannons, I knew they might be killing my loved ones or destroying my home. And there was terrible savagery and ferocity on both sides. When at last I saw my family again, they told me that the grocer's two sons, with whom I had played as a child, had enlisted in the Red Army and had sworn to cut me to ribbons if I fell into their hands.

That war was full of ironies. There was a rich *mujik*, a man who owned a hundred and twenty-five acres, had more than twenty horses, and thirty cattle and much other livestock, in our town. Yet his three sons immediately joined the Reds. One of his neighbors, also a *mujik*, who lived by making Russian ovens, had a wife and seven children, and was as poor as Job. Yet he joined our de-

tachment and fought the entire war in the famous Kornilov regiment.

Several times during this period my life was spared
against all odds. I left my machine gunner's section to join
the cavalry. My grandfather had served Czars Alexander
II, Alexander III and Nicholas II and had retired in 1907
as a general. After his retirement, he had raised horses
and had taught me from the age of two all the skills of a
horseman. So, when it was decided to create a *sotnia*
(mounted section), I was named first officer. I bought a
horse from a former Cossack commander, a beautiful animal but with two faults: he was unwilling to follow other
horses, being used to the lead position, and he was shot
from under me.

After the capture of my *stanitza*, my commander told
me to go back to Ekaterinodar for a few days and not to
stay where everyone knew me. "If the Reds retake the
stanitza," he said, "your relatives may pay dearly for you."

With my orderly, I started back to Ekaterinodar, about
fifty miles away. That evening I arrived at a convent of
nuns located halfway between the stations of Platnirov-
skaya and Platunovskaya. I knew the place very well. The
mother superior, a venerable old lady, had been a great
friend of my grandfather. She told me that the Reds were
burning down all the convents. There was a small Cossack
detachment there, about forty men, on their way to
Ekaterinodar to join the fight, commanded by the sublieutenant Kedrovsky, whom I knew so well.

Like many Russian convents, this one was surrounded

by a high wall and resembled a fortress. My horse had lost a shoe and I sent my orderly to take him to the *stanitza* about three miles away to be reshod. When he left, the massive single gate to the convent was barred and sentinels were placed at the gate and in the bell tower. The front lines were shifting constantly, so that one could expect a Red band at any time. After dinner, the mother superior escorted me to the guest room, while the sublieutenant and his men remained below.

I was sound asleep when firing broke out. A nun woke me at 1 A.M. The Reds had surrounded the convent and Kedrovsky was seriously wounded.

The Cossacks were firing back from the bell towers but we were short of ammunition. Kedrovsky had been carried into the chapel and I could see that he did not have much time left.

"We are done for," he whispered. "There are too many of them. They have two cannons and we only have twenty-five cartridges apiece. Hide. The Cossack troops may be able to save themselves somehow, but for you and me it is certain death. You know how these pigs torture officers. Don't fall into their hands alive."

A Cossack dagger and the nine-millimeter Colt I had received in military school were the only weapons I had. The Red cannons were bombarding the convent and shrapnel was falling everywhere. I left Kedrovsky and went back to the courtyard.

"We can't hold out much longer," a noncommissioned officer told me. "I am going to talk to them. They have promised not to kill us if we open the gate. They don't know you're here. Hide somewhere and no Cossack will betray you."

But where? Surely the Reds would ransack the convent from top to bottom and I would be discovered. I was nineteen, not ready to die. To be killed in battle was one thing, but to kill myself or die under torture was unthinkable.

I shook hands with the sergeant. Kedrovsky had died. The terrified nuns were hiding in the cellars. "I have a place that nobody knows about," the mother superior told me. "My poor daughters are so frightened they might betray you out of fear. You will be safe if the Reds don't stay too long."

She took me to a dark corner of the main church, where there were a number of icons. One icon was very large and so old that nobody knew what saint it represented. The mother superior pressed something at its base, and then drew the icon aside. There was a small cubbyhole where I could just squeeze in. "They won't find you here," she said. "I'll come back when the danger is over. Don't move, and don't smoke."

She moved the icon back in place and I was left in the darkness with only the air that filtered through a small crack in the wall. For a while I listened to the artillery and rifles. It was silent for a brief moment. Then, shots and wild screaming. Afterward, I learned that the Reds had massacred all the Cossacks. Only one, a fellow my own age, had been rescued by the sister-cook, who had hidden him in a dish closet.

The Reds were searching for convent treasure. I heard

them approach with the mother superior. They were warning her that they would kill her if she didn't tell them where it was. They were so close that I could hear their swearwords and their heavy, drunken breathing. They looted the church for about a half hour. In spite of the cold and my cramped quarters, I fell asleep.

I was wakened by someone shaking me and I thought the end had come. When I opened my eyes, I saw some officers and Cossacks, with the mother superior. "Come out of your hole, friend," said a captain I did not know. "And thank the mother superior for saving your life. Everybody else was slaughtered."

I was so stiff I could hardly walk. By the time they got me to the courtyard I saw one of the Cossack detachments from Ekaterinodar. About two hundred Red soldiers had captured the convent as they had been returning from a village where they had looted a State vodka factory. Dead drunk, they had been on their way to the railroad station, where another Red detachment was quartered, when they had come upon the convent and heard that there were Cossacks inside.

While I had slept, the situation had reversed. Exhausted from the fighting and drunk on the mass wine they had looted at the convent, the soldiers, even the sentinels, had fallen asleep. The Cossacks in a nearby *stanitza* had managed to alert a detachment on its way to the front. The battle was short and the Reds were wiped out. Only twenty were left alive to bury the dead, and then they were shot. That was what the Civil War was like.

My orderly returned with my horse, and I set out again for Ekaterinodar.

Despite some victories, our resistance was doomed. There were just a few of us, and masses of Reds were arriving from all sides. We had no reserve ammunition, while the Reds had the leftover reserves of the Russian army at the front.

The noose was tightening around Ekaterinodar. Our superiors — Ataman Filimonov, Colonel Pokrovsky and some generals from the front — decided the only way to escape being annihilated was to retreat to the mountains to the south on the Black Sea. I don't think they had any idea of how we would survive in the mountains or where we would find food for thousands of men. How would we defend ourselves? It was a desperate decision but it was our only choice. The situation became more critical as hordes of civilians and retired officers who were afraid of falling into the hands of the Reds followed us.

In February 1918 we left our beloved city only to run immediately into a line of Bolshevik troops. After a few days of fighting, we were sure the end had come for us. Everyone was put into the front lines, even the civilians and the old men. But toward the evening of the third day somehow we broke through. My mounted detachment had the responsibility of protecting headquarters from a surprise attack.

A horseman galloped out of the woods, leaped from his horse before Ataman Filimonov, and threw his arms around him shouting, "Kornil, Kornil." He was one of our Cherkess allies and had brought us unexpected good news. General Kornilov and his tiny army were just eighteen miles away. We had thought he was still in Rostov-on-the-Don, but he too had evacuated under pressure. He had hoped to join us and wait for better times — for the moment when the Cossacks, who were observing strict neutrality (ninety percent of our men were ex-officers), would understand what real threat the Bolsheviks were to their whole way of life.

Pokrovsky was scheduled to meet Kornilov the next day but Pokrovsky himself had only been named major-general the evening before by Filimonov. This was bound to offend Kornilov and the other generals. Filimonov did not, in their view, have the right to make appointments. Now he had acted as the head of an independent state, and this could only add to the tension between the Cossacks and the Russians. Pokrovsky, because he was not a Cossack, was denied a role in the joined armies.

The meeting of our two small troops under Kornilov's command was to take place in the *stanitza* of Novy-Dmitrievskaya. We hoped to persuade the Cossacks to rise, so we thought it essential to retake their capital, Ekaterinodar. So, at the beginning of March, our army was once again before the city. Ekaterinodar was defended by ten times our strength, and fortified by heavy artillery against our measly ten cannons and two thousand shells. Even so, we might have taken it if General Kornilov had not been hit by a shell. His death was a terrible blow. It overturned all our plans. He was a Cossack general and immensely popular. If we had taken Ekaterinodar, he could have rallied all the Cossacks of Kuban, the Don and Terek. His successor, General Denikine, did not have the same relationship with the men. In any case, he decided to raise the siege and to move us to the territory of the Don Cossacks where, it was rumored, the Cossack contingents had begun to converge.

We went through a village called, in Russian, "The Colonies." It was where the Germans who had been transplanted to Russia under Catherine II lived. With elaborate security, we buried Kornilov. (The next day the Reds discovered his grave and dragged his body through the streets of Ekaterinodar.)

4

Discovery of Fear

BY NIGHT, across the violent winds of the steppes of the northern Caucasus, we marched toward the Don. Each evening as we would start out only the general staff knew what our route was to be. Nevertheless, the Reds succeeded regularly in discovering the *stanitzas* where we halted, and bombarded us with artillery fire. We were so short of guns and shells that we could not fire back except in grave emergency. Our supply corps was the closest Red detachment; when our shells or cartridges ran dangerously low, we raided them.

I took part in these expeditions often. On the steppes of Kuban, one night, we were only a few miles from my village, where my mother and younger brother still lived. I hadn't seen them for months, and was frantic to know if they were all right, but I could not leave the column. I had been assigned to be General Markov's liaison with General Denikine for that night.

It was pitch dark, the clouds blotted out any trace of moonlight, and a cutting wind blew in our faces. We were wearing Cossack *burkas*, long, black felt water- and wind-proof capes which served at night as sleeping bags. We marched eight miles north, then turned south to throw the Bolsheviks off our trail. We had to cross the railroad tracks, a movement which took several hours and was very dangerous since the Reds might easily telephone our position to the armored trains, who could bombard us. To keep the trains from getting too close to the column as it crossed the tracks, teams of sappers would blow up the tracks a few miles away on both sides of our lines.

That night I was following General Denikine's personal bodyguards. Wrapped in my *burka*, I had laid the bridle on the horse's neck and begun to doze off. I was roused when my horse stopped. The column, two or three miles long, had halted and everybody had dismounted. We stretched our stiffened limbs and lay down, covering our heads with our *burkas*. Next to me was a *kurgan*, one of the mounds on which the Cossacks a century before had lit their signal fires to warn of Cherkess attacks. I climbed one side of the *kurgan* to get out of the wind, attached the bridle to my leg to keep my horse from wandering, and fell asleep. After a while, the cold woke me. When I opened my eyes, I leaped up. The column had disappeared. My horse, grazing on the fresh grass, had dragged me gradually down the *kurgan*.

The wind had died and the sky was cloudless. Overhead the moon shone brilliantly; it was absolutely silent. I put my ear to the ground to see if I could pick up any sound of the column and wagons. I could hear nothing. I was quite alone in this vast, dangerous steppe.

I was frozen with such intense fear that I was physically ill. I gave my horse his head in the hopes he would find his own way to our column. I knew the Red cavalry would be close behind. He didn't run, he flew. The noise of his hooves resounded like thunder on the dry ground.

After about an hour, I saw a dark line against the gray horizon. To make less noise, I rode along the side of the road, where the earth was softer. After a while, I realized that the dark line was a row of trees planted along the railway tracks to protect them from snowdrifts. I knew the road would lead to a crossing, but I didn't know what might await me there, so I turned to the right.

When I was five hundred yards from the crossing, I thanked God that I had made a detour. Through the unbearable silence I heard the sound of a train slowly approaching. The armored train, I thought. I dismounted and led my horse into the shadows of the trees. Apparently the Reds had repaired the section of track we had blown up and were searching for the place where we had crossed.

The train had stopped at the crossing house, and I heard what I assumed was the Reds interrogating the railroad guard. I could not distinguish the words. The talking stopped but still the train did not move.

It might stay there until dawn. It was already 3 A.M., so I didn't have much time and the only safety lay on the other side of the tracks. But to cross I would have to go through woods, down along a road that sank three yards below the surrounding ground. The other side was easier. It was only about a yard high, no trouble for my horse. But I would have to do all of this without the men on the train hearing me, and there was no wind to drown out the noise.

I pulled off farther to the right, leading the horse by the bridle. He was used to the front, so we accomplished this easily. Then he saw the tracks glinting in the pale moonlight. I pulled at him with all my strength to get him to cross them. He was afraid of the slippery rails and would not budge. All this effort made a considerable amount of noise.

I could hear my heart beating, and despite the cold I was bathed in sweat. The only solution was to mount the horse, which might lessen his fear and encourage his instinct to obey his rider. I made the sign of the cross and leaped into the saddle and, for the first time ever, struck him with my crop. Surprised and offended, he made such a leap that he almost fell between the tracks, and I had difficulty keeping my mount. Everything happened quickly. I found myself half stunned, lying against a tree. The horse was standing next to me trembling. I could hear the drops of sweat falling from his body onto the ground. My face and hands were scratched from the branches and I had an enormous bump on my head. My whole body hurt but I didn't have time to think. The Reds must certainly have heard. I forced myself to my feet and led the horse through the woods.

A few minutes later, I was on the steppe once again and relieved. I was on the right side. I heard voices from the crossing and then the train began to move. They were searching for the source of the noise. I whipped the horse with my crop and he leaped forward. Immediately, I heard the sound of machine gun fire aimed in the wrong direction. But now the Reds heard the hoof beats on the dry ground. They couldn't get me with a machine gun so they fired a dozen cannon shells. All fell short, except one that landed about two yards to my left.

I galloped God knows where for about twenty minutes. But the horse was about to fall from exhaustion and so I stopped for twenty minutes. I was certain now that the Reds were not going to get me that night. The moon had disappeared behind clouds and a morning fog indicated that I was near a river. My body was aching and the bump on my head was swelling. I stretched out on the ground and heard ahead of me the sound of wagon wheels. "Come on, old friend," I said to my horse, "one more effort and we are home free." The horse, Kochevoi, sensed our friends were near. He let out a whinny that could be heard for miles. A half hour later, I was with my column. By morning we had reached the *stanitza* of Ilinskaya, our next stop on the Don road. I was worried, as I presented myself to the headquarters staff, that I might have been needed during the night to transmit an order to General Markov. There had been nothing. I had not been missed.

Our march was difficult, slowed down by the necessity of pulling the supply wagons, by the civilians who accompanied us, and by the wounded. Since we were always on the move, the wounded could not be properly cared for, and even slight wounds, easily cured in normal circumstances, could be fatal.

In view of the desperate situation, our command decided to leave the wounded behind in Diadkovskaya. At the same time they freed a communist, Polouian, with great ceremony and asked him to watch out for them. I said farewell to the wounded sorrowfully.

Finally, we reached the large *stanitza* of Ourpenskaya, which was near the government seat of Stavropol. This was not a Cossack city and many of its men had joined the Red Army. General Denikine received the news that many Cossacks had risen against the Reds and were ready to join us. Two regiments of Kuban Cossacks arrived. Our situation now seemed a bit hopeful. Denikine decided to march to the Don and soon our army was settled in the two Don Cossack *stanitzas*, Olguiskaya and Metchetinskaya.

The Cossacks of these towns had fought hard against the Reds. They had removed all the tracks that connected the Rostov-on-the-Don to the Ekaterinodar-Tzarizino line. We arrived on the eve of Easter and for the first time in a very long while we had time to celebrate in style.

During the next month we received reinforcements. The situation was looking more favorable. All over the immense empire, groups like ours were forming. Denikine decided to leave the Don and set out on the conquest of the Kuban. It was May, a beautiful month in southern Russia. Our army of ten thousand fighting men started out on the return trip to Kuban. We were glad to get away from the Bolsheviks, at least those in the northern Caucasus. Soon we lost our legendary general, Sergei Leonikovich Markov, a tragedy to us. It happened after we had captured the railroad station of Chablievskaya, on the Novorossisk-Tzarizino line. The battle was virtually over when I saw the general walking between two warehouses. He returned my salute, visibly delighted at this first victory that cut off the Reds from the east. At that moment, a Red shell, fired by the armored train as it retreated, exploded over his head. He died almost immediately. The deaths first of Kornilov then of Markov changed the course of our destiny. Even so, I think that there was never such a small army, almost without resources, that accomplished such exploits against an enemy infinitely superior in numbers, arms and munitions.

A few days after the death of General Markov, I was almost killed during the attack on the Red infantry at the railroad junction of Tichoretskaya. But we captured Tichoretskaya and that opened up the roads to Rostov-on-the-Don and Ekaterinodar and to the southern Caucasus. The Bolsheviks had to abandon an enormous amount of matériel, which we recovered: two armored trains with their battleship guns, hundreds of wagons loaded with ammunition, and many other supplies. The victory also had political significance. It demonstrated our strength to the population, and encouraged those who, even though they hated the Reds, had feared to join us. The arrival of our army in Cossack territory and our victories against the Reds had an immediate result. Everywhere the Cossack *stanitzas* rose against the Communists and our army mushroomed. Day and night, Cossack detachments arrived to join us.

General Pokrovsky was still in disgrace for having accepted promotion by the Ataman Filimonov. He was biding his time. As great numbers of Cossacks began to join us, there was a need for a man like Pokrovsky to command. When he was named commander of the Cossacks, he asked me to be his aide-de-camp, but I chose to join a Cossack detachment serving under him that was commanded by one of my uncles.

Pokrovsky was pitiless with both the Red soldiers and civilians. After we captured Timochevskaya, the people as usual denounced the Bolshevik sympathizers, who were mostly peasants from the interior. He had twenty gallows built and placed in a circle in the main plaza. One stood apart. It was for an officer who had been conscripted by the Reds but who had declared his intention to rejoin our side. When the Reds retreated, he had remained behind and hidden himself. Pokrovsky had him hanged anyhow. Practically all captured officers were hanged. To escape, it was not enough to plead that one had been forced into service. One had to prove that he had acted against the Reds.

On August 2, 1918, a memorable date for me, we entered Ekaterinodar once again after six months' absence. Most of the people gave us a wild welcome. As we marched down the streets they shook our hands and invited the officers to dinner. After this, I received three days' leave to go see my family. I had had no news of them for several months, and I was apprehensive as I approached home. I was overjoyed to find my mother and younger brother well. They had heard from a Cossack who had seen me in Ekaterinodar that I was safe and sound. During the three days we spent together, my mother told me about life under the Bolsheviks. Many of our belongings and household goods had been requisitioned. The Reds had taken all my father's small arms, and even a pair of binoculars he had won in a pistol competition. As he took them, the soldier told my mother that they would be useful in helping aim the cannons against us as we attacked. The essence of civil war is irony: my father's binoculars might have helped kill me.

My mother had not been badly harassed, though my seventeen-year-old brother had been arrested. But he had soon been released after some peasants my mother had once helped intervened. Leaving them was terribly painful. If I had realized that I would end up fighting in a civil war, I would never have joined the army. Now it was too late. "Long farewells bring useless tears," says the Russian proverb. I got on my horse and galloped away to hide my tears.

My regiment was already far away and it took me three days to catch up with it. The rout of the Reds was complete in the northern Caucasus. Cities and *stanitzas* fell to us one after another. Kuban Cossacks, officers, and even soldiers whom the Bolsheviks had not succeeded in converting, flowed into our ranks. We were now one hundred thousand strong. Young as I was, I knew the czarist regime was dead and that Russia needed serious reform — but why must neighbors kill each other, destroy their farms and livestock, and raze their homes?

II

Defeat

5

Farewell Mother Russia

IT IS NOT MY INTENTION to record the history of the Russian Civil War; that has already been done many times. I have recorded these reminiscences of my youth so that my later adventures will be understandable. For two years I fought in numerous battles, was wounded, had four horses shot from under me, and was lucky enough to survive.

Without pretending to be a historian, I would like to suggest why the Army of Volunteers, as we were called, fell short of total victory over the Bolsheviks, even though our victories brought us very close to Moscow. We were so few. We had subdued an immense territory, populated by tens of millions, but our rear was always exposed and could furnish us with no reserves. The orders for general mobilization were ignored. Those who were drafted hid in the forests.

Because we had no real supply system to speak of, we had to live off the population and we made enemies of the

47

people everywhere. If my horse was killed, I had to replace it by requisitioning one from someone who had until then sympathized with us.

The situation with clothing was even worse. For two years I was issued absolutely nothing, and to avoid being eaten alive by lice, I had to requisition whatever I needed from the populace.

The government of the volunteer army issued its own money, called *kolokoltchiki*, but it wasn't worth the paper it was printed on. The population of the conquered areas accepted it only when they had no choice. It is clear why our presence was not always welcome, especially since our victims were usually from among the less well off. The privileged had connections and they could make things hard for us if we bothered them. People who owed their lives to us would complain to the high command about the smallest requisitions.

Lenin, among others, recognized the real reason why we and all the White armies — those of Kolchak, Denikine, Ioudenitch, and later Wrangel — were defeated. So long as our armies were made up of volunteers who were enemies of Bolshevism, everything was all right. But when we had to conscript the peasants and our Red prisoners, our situation became vulnerable.

After coming so close to victory, the volunteer army gave way before the avalanche of the Red forces and their partisans behind our lines. We had few munitions and weapons, and the Allied powers gave us practically nothing. After the French sailors at Odessa mutinied, the Allies were only confirmed in their desire to get out of Russia, where their soldiers might be contaminated by the new ideology.

We could see that the end of Denikine's army was near. I wanted to say what I thought might be a last good-bye to my mother. When I arrived home, I was upset to learn that my brother had enlisted in the guard regiment commanded by my uncle. I had hoped he would stay home to care for my mother. The previous year he had enlisted in another regiment, but I had asked the commander to send him home, since he was a minor and had enlisted without our mother's consent. He had returned, but, as with me, his whole background pressed him into the fight.

Our house was full of refugees, mostly Don Cossacks who had abandoned all their possessions so as not to fall into the hands of the Reds. On my last night home, I invited a few friends and a good accordionist and we spent the evening dancing. About 1 A.M. some Cossacks from our *stanitza* knocked on the door. "Lieutenant," one of them said, "the Reds are only twelve miles away. They'll be here by morning. You must leave right away. They'll kill you if they find you here."

One of them saddled my horse. Six cavalrymen from my regiment had come for me. They had been with me for more than a year, since my last visit home. As I led the horse to the courtyard gate, my mother walked with me. She looked at me for a long time and then blessed me. I kissed her and leaped on my horse so as not to prolong the scene, and galloped off with my Cossacks. Nobody said a word. We had all been through the same drama.

We rode all night in the direction of Ekaterinodar. The

next day, all the roads leading to the city were clogged with refugees and soldiers. The city was unrecognizable. It had been very clean, even pretty. Now it was filthy, crowded with men and horses, and there were drunks everywhere. Our soldiers had pillaged the State-owned vodka factory and everyone, it seemed, had a bottle. I had no idea where to find our regiment, so I decided to press on toward the Black Sea, because I knew that in case of retreat our division would go to Touapse. I said good-bye to my friends. No one knew what the future would be.

We practically had to fight our way across the railroad bridge, which was the only way out of Ekaterinodar in the direction of the mountains. Toward evening we arrived at a large tobacco plant that belonged to a Greek. Some girls who worked in the tobacco curing houses lived in one of the buildings. We asked if we could spend the night with them. I fell madly in love with one of them, a marvelously beautiful young woman. Our idyll lasted only the night and we parted the next morning with breaking hearts.

When I got to Touapse, I learned that my regiment had already passed through, moving toward the Georgia border. Georgia had declared its independence from Russia. I caught up with it at Adler, a tiny and charming village beyond Sotchi.

General Rasstegaev, who commanded my regiment, told me that it was now part of a cavalry brigade of which he was to take command. He made me his adjutant because I was good at writing reports and orders. But the appointment was meaningless; a few days later the brigade had ceased to exist.

The mountain forests surrounding us were filled with

Red partisans, the "Greens," who attacked continuously, while the 9th Red Army pressed us from the coast. Our Cossacks were increasingly demoralized.

Now, we were ordered to Georgia, where we would certainly be disarmed and interned according to international law. The brigade was assembled and the order given to move toward the border, a few miles away. The general turned his head only to discover that half the brigade had not budged. He galloped back, with me following.

"What are you doing here? Didn't you hear my orders?" he shouted at them. The general began to curse them, castigating them for their disobedience. It was a dangerous game to provoke three hundred Cossacks who were afraid of nothing or nobody.

The only officer with them was a young lieutenant, a good friend of mine. At last he came forward and saluted his commander. "General, we have decided not to go to Georgia. We prefer to wait here and surrender to the Red Army."

The general's face turned crimson. Without a word, he wheeled on his horse, rode over to those who had followed him, and ordered them to return to their lodgings. I knew that he was deeply humiliated. Not only had the Cossacks refused to obey him, but the lieutenant and at least fifty of them were from his own *stanitza*.

An hour later, a cargo ship dropped anchor a good way from shore; Adler had no harbor. The sea was very rough, and a small boat lowered from the ship had a terrible time getting to shore.

I went out to meet the landing party and asked what

they had come for. The ship's second officer replied that they had been sent to pick up as many men as possible and take them to the Crimea. "But," he added, "we cannot take any horses. We have no way of loading them, and besides, we are anchored practically in the open sea."

The general asked his Cossacks whether they would agree to embark for the Crimea without their horses. Their answer was immediate and unanimous; they would rather go to Georgia. At that point, the general made a mistake that cost him his command and his commission. Overwhelmed by betrayal, he wanted only to get away as soon as possible.

"Pity, I shall leave alone, and you will accompany me," he said to me, "but I absolutely demand that they take our horses." He explained to the second officer that they were thoroughbreds that could not be left to the Bolsheviks. The officer agreed but only at our own risk. It took five hours to get the horses on board, and they were so frightened and exhausted that they took a week to recover.

When we arrived at Theodosia, an ancient city founded by the Greeks, we presented ourselves to General Babiev, commander of the Cossack division. Shortly afterward, Rasstegaev was dismissed for having abandoned his Cossacks. (I saw him years later in Paris, singing for tips in a cabaret. I was too embarrassed to speak to him.)

I was sent to the famous Wolf regiment, which had been established during the Civil War by General Schkouro. I was not held in blame, since it was assumed that I had had to follow the general's orders. A few days later, most of the Cossacks still at Adler were evacuated to

Theodosia without their horses. Those who did not follow the general were conscripted into the Red Army.

Without their horses, the Cossacks had lost their souls. Fortunately, new mounts were found for them two months later. General Denikine was forced to resign his command. The head of the new "Russian Army" was General Piotr Nikolaevitch, Baron Wrangel. A very cultivated man, he had been a mining engineer before becoming a soldier, and had studied at the famous Nicolas Cavalry School at St. Petersburg and later at the War College, where he had finished first in his class. During World War I he had won the Cross of St. George for having captured a German battery at the head of his squadron. During the Civil War he commanded the Cossack divisions and was very popular. He was the most liberal of all our generals and the most hated by the Bolsheviks, who called him the "Black Baron." They judged correctly that his very liberalism made him the most dangerous of their enemies. Alone among the White generals, he had a program for the future of Russia, if his troops should be victorious. He abolished reprisals against Red prisoners and forbade requisitions from the civilian population. But he had come to command too late, and he knew it.

Immediately after he took command, he began to work out plans to evacuate the troops abroad in case of defeat. He made arrangements with the French government, the only foreign power that recognized his authority.

Although he took the precaution of planning for a possible evacuation, Wrangel was not a man to give up without a fight. His plan was to break out of the peninsula and try to incite an insurrection while the Reds were having trouble on the Polish front. But his calculations left out one essential consideration: the Russian people could not forgive Wrangel for his foreign family alliances.

During this new brief war, I had another proof of my extraordinary luck. Early in May of 1920, a week before our army broke out of the Crimea, I had been in the trenches with my regiment, facing the Red lines. One morning, the commander had ordered me to take a few Cossacks that night and try to capture prisoners.

Between our lines and the Reds there was a wide no-man's-land where there were nightly skirmishes between reconnaisance parties. I chose a few Cossacks whom I knew to be adept at this kind of operation and we worked out a plan. To kill time during the afternoon, as we waited, I played a few hands of cards and won quite a lot of money. By evening, however, I was ill with chills and a high fever. When it was time to set out, I was running a temperature of 104. I could not possibly go on such a mission. Another officer went in my place. In the morning we learned that the reconnaisance party had fallen into an ambush and no one had returned.

My illness was diagnosed as typhus. It left me completely exhausted; nonetheless, it had saved my life. I was sent away for a month's convalescence, and then rejoined my regiment.

When General Wrangel realized that his offensive against the superior Red forces was doomed, he took a long shot. That was when he decided to invade part of the Kuban Cossack territory, hoping to stir the population against the Bolsheviks, of whom they had, by this time, some experience. His hopes were illusory. This was the last offensive of the White Army — and it was the battle that claimed the life of my younger brother.

Only the Cossack regiments were to invade Kuban from the coast of the Azov Sea, but our preparations were apparently known to the Reds well in advance. The landing was to take place near the *stanitza* of Primorsko-Akchtarskaya on the eastern shore of the Azov Sea. The landing was easy, following a short bombardment of the shore. This was the last time I saw my brother. His regiment, formerly the personal guard of the Czar, was the first to set out on a landing barge. My regiment was to follow close behind. My last sight of him was as he stood in the prow of the landing barge, smiling and waving to me.

As we should have expected, the landing was a fiasco. The Cossack population did not budge. Those whom the Bolsheviks considered bad risks had been removed before we landed. In any case, the Cossacks had not forgotten their grievances against the White Army. There is a Russian proverb that says, "Never spit in a well; you may need to drink from it someday."

For the first time, we were facing a new Red Army, better outfitted and equipped than we were. It was clear from the start that they were unbeatable. On the evening of August 22, the day my brother was killed, the First Cossack division, commanded by General Babiev, arrived at the *stanitza* of Olguinskaya, with a great number of Red prisoners. Almost immediately, he had to order us out, without a chance to rest either ourselves or our exhausted horses. He had been informed that the Red cavalry was attempting to cut us off from our base. With us were two companies from the Konstantin Military School of Kiev and two cannons. He left only two sections of my regiment, my own included, in the *stanitza*, along with the cadets and the two cannons.

We were glad of a chance to catch some sleep. But we had also been left in charge of a few hundred prisoners, and we didn't know what to do with them. They were mostly boys of eighteen to twenty who did not understand the war at all. We couldn't let them go nor could we kill them. Soon, our dilemma was solved for us. A patrol, coming in from the opposite direction General Babiev had gone in, notified us that a large force of Red cavalry was advancing toward the *stanitz*a. Since cavalry cannot fight in a town, the director of the military school, the highest-ranking officer among us, ordered us to withdraw immediately to the north, in the direction of our landing base. We had to abandon the prisoners.

Our cavalry detachment left the *stanitza* last. A little over a mile from the village, we spotted a full Red cavalry regiment facing the village from the east. When they saw us, they advanced in attack formation.

We were only about a hundred and fifty and would be overrun easily without even the chance to resist with honor. All we could do was retreat, and even then our chances of getting away were almost nil. We knew what would happen to us: the officers would be slaughtered and the Cossacks taken prisoner.

When the Reds were about five hundred yards from us,

they broke into a full gallop. We drove our horses to the utmost of their endurance but the Reds' horses were in much better condition, and they gained on us. They were now only a hundred yards away. Behind me, I saw that the front rider had seen my epaulets and had picked me out. His saber was extended.

My horse was slowing down. I put my sword away and took out my pistol. I would take a few Reds, and use the last bullet on myself. My orderly's horse fell just in front of me. There was nothing I could do for him. The Red horseman was still behind me. Though he wore no insignia, he was clearly the leader of the regiment. I fired twice and missed. But the third time, I saw him fall less than fifty yards behind me.

We were all resigned to die — and then we were miraculously rescued. The two companies of cadets, who had been hidden by a tall growth of sunflowers, were suddenly visible, and getting ready to fire on the Red cavalry. One company formed the first line, kneeling on one knee, and behind it stood the second. On their flanks were two heavy Maxim machine guns. They waited for us to get close. As soon as we had spotted them, our two detachments split in two, going off to the right and the left.

The Reds were practically on top of us, charging with such screams and curses that even seasoned soldiers would have been terrified, but the students did not move a muscle. Then came a curt order, and all hell broke loose. The Red horsemen, cut down by the rifle and machine-gun fire, turned back. Our two cannons had been brought up in the rear and they opened fire on them as they fled.

The field was filled with dead and wounded men and horses. It was an incredible experience in every way: the courage and coolness of the students; the savagery of the Red attack, its courage and fanaticism. We learned later that there had been three regiments against our two companies. But such defeats were of no use now. It had been over for us ever since the failure of our ill-advised landing.

We were ordered to the coast, where boats were waiting to take us back to the Crimea. I asked about my brother's regiment and was told it was due in an hour. I went under a tree to wait. The heat was unbearable. I was terribly anxious and went out to the road to watch, hiding myself behind shrubs. At last, in the distance was the glorious standard of His Imperial Majesty that had been awarded to the regiment for its valor in the battle of Leipzig in 1813. My grandfather, father, uncles, cousins, my brother and I myself had all served under it.

The regiment had almost passed by and there was still no sign of my brother. Then I saw Berejnoi, his friend, a boy of the same age who had volunteered at the same time. I called to him and he came toward me. His manner was enough to tell me what I feared to hear. "Where is Ivan?" For a long moment he did not answer. "He was killed the day before yesterday." I had been waiting for these words, but they struck me like a blow in the face. Berejnoi told me how Ivan had died, and that he had been buried with another officer and two Cossacks in the *stanitza* of Grivenskaya with full military honors. Some of his belongings had been kept for me.

My brother's death affected me so that I could not bear

the idea of going back to war. When I got back to the Crimea, I told my commander that I had to have some time off. He consented, and I returned to Theodosia with a small detachment of veterans of the Civil War. I was then twenty-two years old.

The news from the front was very pessimistic. Under pressure from the Reds, the army had been forced to retreat to the Crimea, which was protected by fortifications, some built by the Tartars and some by us. Our army thought they had foreseen everything, but the fierce cold was a surprise — and a costly one. The only unfortified part of the Crimea was along the stormy Sivach Bay, which was on the army's right flank and was to have formed an invulnerable barrier against the Reds. But the supposedly unpassable Sivach froze overnight so thick that the Red cavalry crossed it easily and attacked from the rear. That was the end of the White Army.

6

Into Exile

SO, NOW I WAS ON BOARD the steamboat *Vladimir* as it got under way to leave Theodosia. The Black Sea is often stormy in the winter, but that November day it was extraordinarily calm. It seemed to me that even the sea understood the tragedy of men about to leave their homeland forever.

The good weather lasted all the way to Constantinople, which was lucky because many of the boats were old and all were overloaded. Even a slight storm could have caused a catastrophe. That night there was a cold wind and I pushed my way below deck, but the air was so stale I couldn't stand it for more than five minutes. I found a small space on deck amid all the heads and legs, wrapped myself in my *burka*, and for the first time in my life, fell asleep outside my homeland.

In the morning the cold was intense. The waves were higher, and the boat began to pitch. On the horizon we could see a large two-stack ship and near it a smaller ship.

Small boats were passing between them. The smaller ship, the *Caucasus*, terribly overloaded with men, was slowly sinking. Fortunately, it stayed afloat until all on board had been evacuated.

The sun rose higher and warmed us somewhat. I was terribly hungry. Before we had left shore I had been able to find a large can of English corned beef, but no one had been willing to sell us any bread, since they knew that our money would be worthless after we departed. I opened the can with my Cossack dagger and began to eat with my fingers. When I saw the haggard faces of the others, and how they gazed at my every mouthful, I offered to share the meat with the men around me. One of them had a few pieces of bread and we ate that with the canned meat. It was very spicy and made us frightfully thirsty. One man volunteered to go for water. It took him an hour to fight his way through the crowd and return with a bucket of foul-smelling water that we drank with pleasure.

To pass the time, I decided to search the ship for friends. I received nothing but hostile looks since I had to trample on people's feet in order to move. The men were used to the worst after two years of civil war, but it was particularly difficult for the few women on board.

At last I found some officers from my former regiment near the prow. Because we were facing into the wind it was colder there than on the decks, but also less crowded. We made a sort of tent around ourselves to block the wind and stayed there together. The next day we saw some low mountains split by a deep crevasse, the entrance to the

Bosporous straits. On both sides stood the ruins of forts that no longer threatened anybody. Turkey had lost the war and Constantinople was occupied by French, English and Italian troops.

In front of us and behind us, ships of our armada waited for permission to enter the straits. Mixed in with great ships like the *Don*, the *Rion*, and the *Kherson* there were smaller boats of every description, about a hundred altogether. Anything that could float had been used in the evacuation.

As our ship entered the Bosporus, I forgot my troubles and the hunger and cold. There was Asia on one side, and Europe on the other. At the Golden Horn, I could scarcely contain myself. On the left was Scutari, in front of Istanbul with its dome of Sancta Sophia and the minarets of hundreds of mosques. Our whole armada was assembled in the strait, accompanied by warships of the occupying powers. Not far off was the magnificent cruiser, the *General Kornilov*, and the elegant yacht, the *Loucoul*, which carried General Wrangel, his family and staff. The *General Kornilov*, pride of the Russian navy, which had been launched in 1915, was to be taken by the French to Bizerte, where it rotted away because the French refused to return it to the Soviet Union. The *Loucoul* later sank in the Bosporus.

The noonday sun made us forget the freezing cold of Russia. As soon as we cast anchor we were surrounded by small boats filled with Greek and Turkish merchants selling all kinds of supplies. Almost nobody had any foreign money, of course. For a loaf of bread or a kilo of figs, the vendors would take a wedding ring. One could buy some bread and some halvah for a pistol. The goods and payments were raised and lowered in nets over the side of the ship. To persuade us to deal with them rather than the Turks, the Greeks would make the sign of the cross in the Orthodox fashion. Most of us on the boats had eaten nothing for three days and many gave away anything they had for some bread. I had two automatic pistols, a gold watch, a gold cigarette case, my dagger with its silver handle, and a gold cross and chain that my mother had given me. It was all I owned in the world, and in spite of my hunger, I could not part with my possessions.

Shortly afterward, I was glad I had made that decision. A motor launch was headed for us loaded with bread. Because there was not enough to go around, the crew began throwing the bread up onto the deck; but the railings were high and a good deal fell into the water. It made me feel sick to see this food being lost, so I gazed instead at the city's panorama. Suddenly, out of nowhere, a magnificent loaf of bread, which must have weighed almost a pound, landed in my arms. I finished it off in short order and began to feel more optimistic. It is amazing what a loaf of bread can do for a hungry man.

Alongside the small boats of the merchants, there were other small craft pulling up. These held families of officers who had been evacuated a month or two earlier, searching for husbands, fathers and brothers. It was an almost impossible task, and even if they did find them, it was still useless. We were forbidden by the Allies to disembark.

In the evening the sailors told us that our ship was

lifting anchor and that we would be put off on some Greek island. Eventually we learned that the island was Lemnos in the Aegean Sea, populated by a few very poor people. It did not seem a very cheerful prospect. As we got into the open sea, the boat began to pitch wildly and many were seasick.

As we passed through the Dardanelles the next day, we saw the wreck of the French heavy cruiser, the *Bove*, which had been sunk by a mine during the world war. Toward evening we made out the outline of our "promised land," as one compatriot called it. The land looked gray and sterile. It made me melancholy.

They put us off in groups on a peninsula that was connected to the island by a narrow isthmus. The peninsula had been an Allied naval base during the world war. There was a large building that desalinated seawater, and next to it some wooden barracks. Farther on stood an immense wooden warehouse, its walls painted with pitch, and beyond that some houses that must have been occupied by the headquarters staff during the war. Far off on the right we could see the Greek city of Moudros, and on the other side of the isthmus was the village of Portianos.

We were each given bread and a can of pâté, and were issued tents large enough to hold ten men. Soon a city of tents arose and the place looked less forbidding. It was terribly cold and we shivered inside the tents, though they were secure and quite waterproof.

Exhausted, we soon fell asleep, but around midnight we were awakened by an uproar — shouting and the sound of wood being ripped apart. The Cossacks, frozen inside their tents, were dismantling the warehouse, the only wood on the island. We took our share. By morning, the warehouse had disappeared. We forgot one detail, however. The planks were coated with pitch and let off a suffocating black smoke when burned.

As the days went by, the camp took on the appearance of a real city, but it was only appearance. There was nothing inside — no source of heat, no beds or covers, no water to wash ourselves or our clothes. Crowded together, we were soon infested by an enormous army of lice, which we could not fight off. It was a horrible existence.

Our legal situation was also precarious. When General Wrangel realized that his army could no longer resist the Red Army, he had appealed to foreign governments to aid the refugees when they left the Crimea. Poland had just concluded an agreement with the Reds, and that had freed the Red Army to fight Wrangel. But, during a dangerous time for Poland, when Boudienny's Red cavalry was advancing on Warsaw, Wrangel had helped the Poles by breaking out of the Crimea and marching toward the Ukraine. To show its gratitude on behalf of its Polish ally, the French government had given de jure recognition to the Crimean government. Therefore, it was normal enough for Wrangel to appeal to France to save the lives of his followers. The French agreed to assist the refugees until they could migrate to new homelands.

The French commissary supplied us with daily food: a loaf of bread for every five persons (shipped all the way from Constantinople, it was almost inedible by the time it arrived), a can of corned beef for every four people, a spoonful of margarine each, and a little sugar and tea. We put everything except the sugar and tea into a large pot and this "soup" was our daily nourishment. It left us chronically hungry.

But the French did not neglect their own interests. They confiscated all the Russian ships as well as all their supplies. This caused terrible privation. They ordered the Cossacks shipped to Lemnos and the regular detachments to near Gallipoli. The situation of the regulars was even worse than ours; the land there was an absolute desert. To keep us from escaping, the French treated us not as allies but as prisoners of war.

There were some English soldiers and one officer on Lemnos, charged with dismantling their base, but their barracks were some distance away and we saw little of them. Our sources told us that one could get all sorts of supplies in the Greek village, from which we were cut off. I wracked my brain to find a way of getting there. There came a day when I was so hungry that I decided to give it a try, come what might. I would have to cross through the English zone and then pass the posts of the Cherkess, who were guarding us for the French. Since I didn't have a penny to my name, I took along an Austrian pistol that I had captured. In Western Europe, if someone offered a gun to a grocer, he would call the police. But, in the East, a pistol is the easiest thing in the world to sell.

I knew that the only safe way out was right through the English encampment and I thought if I could get through there, I wouldn't have to worry about the Cherkess guards. I passed the barracks without seeing a soul, and I was sure that I was safely on the open road when I heard footsteps gaining on me. I decided to head for an outdoor privy I saw nearby, but as soon as I was inside realized that I had made a mistake. Through a crack in the door I could see an English officer heading straight for the privy, and for me.

He approached and I heard him swear when he saw that it was occupied. First come, first served, I said to myself. I waited for him to go away. Unfortunately, that was not his attitude. He kept pounding on the door and swearing. After a few minutes, I realized I had no choice and opened the door. When he saw me, he got so angry I thought he was going to hit me. The only thing I could think to do was draw my pistol and say "Russian officer." He got the message and backed off. I also backed away until I had passed the barracks and the way was open. Later, I learned that the privy was "for officers only," and that, although he was the only officer in the detachment, British military discipline allowed no exceptions.

In the village I was astonished to see the main street lined with shops. I went into what looked like the best of the lot and was overwhelmed by the variety of the merchandise. I wondered who in this poor village could afford all these preserves, canned meats, honey, and chocolate. Soon I realized that all these goods were a burden to the proprietor. Only a short time before, there had been a sizable English garrison nearby with plenty of money to spend. When they departed, the merchants were left high and dry. So, my entrance was greeted with warm smiles and handshakes.

Before offering my pistol for sale, I asked the prices of

some of the goods. After I had figured out how much I wanted would cost, I decided on three hundred drachmas for my Austrian pistol. The merchant, as I had foreseen, was anxious to bargain and made a counteroffer of two hundred. After some haggling, we agreed on two hundred and fifty, and I chose what I wanted. I was so hungry that I couldn't wait until I got back to camp. I ate two cans of sardines, some salmon, ham, and chocolates so fast that the Greek merchant could barely believe his eyes.

In the evening I made my way back to camp without incident, and shared some of my food with my companions, who had not expected me to come back with such treasure. From then on I was the go-between between the village and camp. My comrades awaited my arrival with impatience. One day they told me about a Russian soldier who lived in a nearby village. I asked to meet him and two days later they introduced us. He was a sailor, not a soldier, and had been wounded during the war and cared for in the English hospital. By the time he was well, the Revolution had broken out, and he had married a Greek woman and settled down on the island.

Since he spoke Greek quite well, he was a great help to me as an interpreter. He advised me that pistols were very much in demand and that I had been selling mine much too cheaply. A few days later, I arrived in town with three pistols and asked a thousand drachmas apiece. The merchants pointed to their foreheads to indicate that I must be mad. I walked out of the store. At the edge of the village they caught up with me and the real bargaining began. Two hours later, we had agreed on eight hundred drachmas per pistol.

At this point the English soldiers left the island, and the Cherkess guards took over the part of the line they had been covering. This made getting through much more difficult, but for a while I was able to slip through between two outposts. By now I was obsessed with the idea of escaping. My sailor friend told me that there were several bands of Greek smugglers. If I paid them well enough, they could get me to Greece or Turkey. I had no money, but I still had my gold cigarette case, which weighed two grams. I asked my friend to introduce me to them.

The smugglers were enough to strike fear into the heart of the timid. They were big, rough men, windburned from the open sea. They invited us to share their meal and we accepted. After eating and prodigious drinking, they fell to singing. When that was over, the serious conversation between the "captain" and me began. To my great surprise, he spoke Russian. He had been born in Odessa and had lived there until he was twenty-five. He had had to leave the city in a hurry to escape arrest for killing a customs official. When I heard his story, I decided not to trust myself to his mercies, but I continued the negotiations. I told him I had no money but that I owned a gold cigarette case. He was pleased, until I told him that I had left it in the camp and would show it to him when we met next. He didn't much like that, but agreed to take me to Salonika in two weeks, since he was going there on business.

When we left, I told my sailor friend that I would never dare to go to sea with those ruffians. He insisted that I was wrong to judge them on their appearances, that they were honest men in spite of their trade. I decided to postpone my decision until the next meeting. I had a little reserve of provisions, so I delayed a few days before returning to the village.

Three days later, an old colonel whom I had known for a long time came to me. He was dying of hunger, he said, because he couldn't digest the rations issued to us. He offered me his Mauser and asked me to trade it in the village for something he could eat. I could not refuse this old, sick man the opportunity to eat some decent food before he died. I promised to go.

I got there without any problem and sold his pistol easily, since he had also supplied some cartridges, a very scarce item. I bought some food for him I was sure he would like, and on the way home I was thinking about how pleased he would be. But when I arrived at my usual crossing point, I found an outpost manned by three Cherkess soldiers. Whichever direction I went, I found more guards. It was getting later and later, and I knew things would be even worse in the morning.

One side of the small peninsula where our camp was located faced the open sea, but the other side was bounded by a bay where the water was relatively shallow and calm when the wind blew from the land. That night the wind was blowing from the center of the island. I crept to the shore and found the water was very cold but shallow enough to walk in. I still had about a mile to go to reach the camp. I packed the colonel's supplies and my clothes around my shoulders and waded in. I walked out to about ten yards from the shore; nobody could see me from shore. The water was up to my chest. I was frozen.

About halfway across, the wind suddenly changed. It began to blow into my face. The waves were over my head. The undertow grew stronger and I began to lose my footing. At this point, the shore was rocky and forbidding, and I couldn't climb out of the water. I thought of ditching the colonel's foodstuffs and my clothes. But where could I find new clothing — I decided to fight it out. Once more, Lady Luck came to my rescue. The wind suddenly shifted. I slowly made my way to a safe part of the shoreline and later reached camp, frozen and exhausted but alive.

Our situation was more desperate with each passing day. With the hunger and cold, the increasing filth of our clothing and living quarters, many of the Cossacks and officers began to think they would die on that miserable island. We were told that General Wrangel had gone to Bulgaria and Yugoslavia to ask asylum for his soldiers. Meanwhile, the French had announced their intention to cut off their aid to the refugees. Shortly they showed their hand: "Enlist in the Foreign Legion and your future will be secure." France had a Moroccan war on its hands and needed experienced soldiers. Many Cossacks enlisted, and some returned to Russia to take their chances there rather than die on Lemnos or in North Africa.

7

Flight from Lemnos

I WOULD NOT ENLIST in the legion, but neither could I return to Russia. I would certainly be hanged on the spot. I kept trying to think of some way to escape, and I would certainly have ended up going with the smugglers if some good news had not reached us at last. General Wrangel had obtained the agreement of the Yugoslav government to accept the women, children, sick, wounded and elderly refugees on Lemnos. A ship was to come for them in a few days. Of course, I didn't belong to any of the groups that were to be evacuated.

When the day of departure dawned, a huge Russian ship, the *Kherson*, appeared on the horizon. It was too large to get close to the island and a small Greek boat was brought out to ferry the passengers. A crowd began to gather very early in the morning and boarding was set for 9 A.M. Since I had nothing better to do, I went down to watch. The arrangements were being supervised by the Russian commander who, when he saw me, whispered: "Nicholas, do you want to get out of this place?"

"Do I? But how?"

"Take a piece of paper out of your pocket and pretend to show it to me. I'll pass you onto the ferry. When you get aboard, hide until it's time to board the *Kherson*. From there on, you're on your own."

I looked for a hiding place on the ferry. The decks and cabins were full; I would have to go down into the hold. The first hold was too close to the deck to be safe, but, as I searched, I found a small opening in a corner. This led to a lower hold which would, I thought, make a safe hiding place. So I climbed down the iron ladder into the darkness. I couldn't see a thing. I felt around me and came on some empty crates. I sat down on one of them.

Suddenly, I heard something move nearby and then something brushed against me. Rats. I tried to build a barricade around myself with the crates, and then I sat down with my back against the hull. I had thought they would leave me alone, but I was wrong. The rats attacked me from all sides. Picking up a plank, I began to swing left and right, but this only served to madden them. Several jumped on my legs and bit me before I could knock them off.

I was so desperate I almost called out. At that moment, the ship's engines started up and I would not have been heard, in any case. I found another plank and with the two of them I battled the rats for a quarter of an hour that seemed like an eternity. I could feel the plank hitting against what seemed like a carpet of rats but they kept jumping onto my legs and biting me.

Then the boat slowed down, and a few minutes later it

stopped altogether. I made my way toward the ladder, literally walking on rats and kicking them out of the way; as I climbed up the ladder two of them still clung to my legs. At last I reached the upper hold and then got onto the deck. I was safe but everybody was staring at me; there was blood all over my hands and legs.

The Greek captain saw immediately what had happened to me. I explained my dire situation to him in French, and he took me to his cabin, where he washed and disinfected my wounds. After he had bandaged them, he urged me to seek medical help on board the *Kherson*. What he had been able to do was inadequate, and my wounds were likely to become infected. And rats can carry the plague.

As soon as I reached the deck of the *Kherson*, I was taken charge of by a nurse, who led me to the infirmary. The ship's doctor examined me all over as I told him what had happened. He had my clothes burned and told me to wash thoroughly. What a pleasure it was to put on clean clothes again. Under the attentive care of the nurses, I began to revive.

I tried not to think of the future; how would I survive in foreign countries where I knew nobody? I had no job skills and not a penny in my pocket.

On the morning of December 31, 1920, the *Kherson* pulled into an inlet between some mountains. Passing through the Gulf of Kotor we steamed into the great harbor of Katarro. In front of us was Mount Lovtchen, on which was perched the kingdom of Montenegro; to our right, in the distance, we could see Albania. We gradually approached the little port of Zelenika, where we were to disembark.

The cafés and restaurants reminded me that I was hungry. I didn't want to sell any of my "treasures" but I had been given some slippers on the ship and I was carrying my new English leather boots in a sack. I put them on sale in a café. After a little haggling, I had a hundred crowns in my pocket. As I left the café, I ran into a captain whom I had known quite well. He had fifty dinars. Pooling our resources, we had enough to celebrate the New Year in style. We went to a café that was frequented by Russian refugees, most of them wounded officers like my friend the captain. They invited us to join them, and then the drinking began. We drank to our country and to a quick return; we drank really to forget our exile and the uncertain future. I drank so much that I do not remember how I ended up in a barracks with my friend. But I had nothing to fear. No one asked me any questions and I was put on the list to receive free food and four hundred dinars a month. The king of Yugoslavia welcomed us like brothers. Later, all the Cossacks on Lemnos were evacuated to Yugoslavia, where many of them were assigned to border patrols. Many Russian officers and physicians were able to find positions in Yugoslavia that resembled what they had had in Russia.

My leg wounds were a source of concern. They were healing very slowly and the treatments I received from a Russian doctor did not seem to help much. I was also worried about proper clothing. After my clothes had been burned on the *Kherson*, I had been given some that had been disinfected so often that they smelled to high heaven. They were also too small for me. My captain friend told me that there was a warehouse of civilian clothes in Zelenika sent by the American Red Cross.

I went to see Mr. Rodzianko, the head of the Russian Red Cross in Zelenika, but to my surprise I was refused any help. I was so angry that I began to plan my revenge on him and, at the same time, get what I needed. Each week we went in groups to baths, which were next to a deep and rapid creek that ran down from the mountains. We entered the baths from the side away from the creek, there we left our shoes and hats. Then we went into a large room on the creek side, where we took off our clothes, made a package out of them, and put them inside a steam cylinder to be disinfected. After we bathed, we emerged on the other side, where we found our shoes and hats and retrieved our clothing from the opposite end of the steam cylinder.

After I undressed, I waited for everyone else to go into the baths. I made a pack of my clothes and put two heavy stones inside it. Stark naked, I walked back out and threw the bundle into the creek. Then I went into the bath, washed thoroughly, and came out with all the others to wait for my clothes to be taken out of the disinfectant. When they didn't turn up, I began to protest loudly and to complain of the cold. I was given a blanket while everyone searched high and low for my clothes. It soon became clear that they would not be found. An attendant was dispatched to Rodzianko, who finally relented. I was issued clean underclothing and a splendid suit. The label in one of the pockets read, "Wood & Saxe, Tailors, New York."

That was one thing solved. There remained the problem of my legs, which were giving me more and more trouble. The camp physician sent me to the hospital in Ragusa (today Dubrovnik), which was located in an enormous former convent with endless corridors and rooms of every size and shape. The physician in charge was the former chief medical officer of the Austrian army and there was also a Russian doctor. Soldiers of the new Kingdom of the Serbs, Croats, and Slovenes served as nurses. I spent a month there and was very well taken care of. Toward the end of my stay, I learned that my uncle, the colonel of the former Escort of the Czar, now called the Kuban guard, was also in Yugoslavia.

I was just getting ready to leave the hospital when I became deathly ill. Two days before I was to leave, I had gone to the toilet at night with almost no clothes on. The hospital had no electric light after 10 P.M. There were small alcohol lamps in the rooms but no light at all in the corridors. The toilets were quite far from my room and I got lost in the unlit corridors. I was terribly cold and I called out to the nurse but the place was so huge that I wandered for almost an hour before anyone heard me. I was trembling like a leaf. In the morning I had a high fever and developed pneumonia. For two weeks I was between life and death. Even after the fever had passed, it took me two weeks to recover my strength. I had to stay in the hospital another month.

Finally I was discharged from the hospital. The administration gave me a new civilian suit, a little money, and a ticket to the city of Novi Sad, where my uncle was living. His wife had left Russia to join him three months earlier with their son and two daughters. Novi Sad had belonged until recently to Hungary and had three names — Novi Sad in Serbian, Neusatz in German, and Újvidék in Hungarian — and its population was as mixed as its names. The children playing in the streets spoke not only three national languages but also Yiddish, for there was also a sizable Jewish population. It was a wonderfully charming city on the Danube.

My aunt was an enterprising woman. She had managed to save her valuable jewels and with the money had bought a hotel with a superb café. (Two years later, she and one of her partners lost control of the establishment to the third partner. But in the meanwhile, I lived the high life.) I had the best room in the hotel; I ate in the café and my aunt gave me pocket money. She bought me two new suits in the latest fashion. It was a soft life, but I was uneasy living off my relatives. So one day I decided to go to Belgrade in search of any former comrades who might be there. Belgrade had suffered terribly during the war from bombardment by the Austrians across the Danube. Rebuilding was going on everywhere.

After several days in Belgrade I was involved in a dramatic incident and my good luck saved me once again. The parliament building had been renovated and was to be dedicated by the prince regent, the future King Alexander. He was to be accompanied by President Pašić. I found a spot along the parade route near a large building where construction work was going on. In order to see over the mounted guards along the street, I stood on a small pile of bricks. I could hear the cheering in the distance and then the church bells began to ring. There was a foreigner standing next to me, a man of medium height who could not see over the guards. Since I was tall enough to see the parade from ground level, I gave him my place on the pile of bricks. The parade came along and I could see the regent and Pašić, seated in an open carriage.

After that, things happened so quickly I couldn't tell what was going on. The horses fell under their traces; there were people covered with blood. The police were running in all directions. There had been an assassination attempt against the regent. The foreigner next to me was stretched out on the ground, his face covered with blood. As I tried to reach him, the police arrived and carried him to an ambulance. Next day I read in the newspapers that he was Swiss and had been hit by a bomb fragment. He had been blinded. Given my height, the shrapnel would have hit me in the chest if I had stayed standing on the bricks.

III

The Treasure of the White Army

8

A Fantastic Secret

AT THE RUSSIAN EMBASSY in Belgrade I ran into a fellow officer who had been attached to the same brigade as I at the outbreak of the Civil War. I had not laid eyes on him since those days.

"My dear friend," he said, "you are just the man I have been looking for. Of course, I had no idea I would find you here though I knew you were in Yugoslavia. I have just returned from Bulgaria, and I had a talk with General Pokrovsky in Sofia. He asked me to try to find you and to set up a meeting with him there. Here is a ticket. His address is marked on the back."

I was startled. I had not even seen the general for ages and had never felt sympathetic toward him. I disapproved of his cruelty to the enemy and, as well, his behavior toward the Cossacks. Why on earth would he wish to see me? Out of curiosity, and because I was bored and wanted to do something new, I decided to go anyhow.

I went back to Novi Sad to tell my aunt and uncle.

They tried to dissuade me from going without being quite sure why. My uncle knew Pokrovsky and didn't think highly of him. But I had made up my mind, and two days later, I took the train for Sofia. I didn't have a passport, but I managed to get through both the Serbian and the Bulgarian customs with a sort of identification that my uncle had written out on some of his leftover regimental letterhead.

When I arrived at Pokrovsky's house, his orderly informed me that the general was in Tirnovo, the former capital of the Bulgarian kingdom. The next day I found him in a house on the outskirts of the city. It belonged to a Bulgarian colonel who was an adversary of the government. Pokrovsky greeted me warmly: "I am delighted to see you, *molodoi* [young man]. I'll tell you later why I sent for you. First, let's go eat. But forget the General Pokrovsky. I am incognito here. I am Captain Ivanov."

The political situation in Bulgaria was complicated. Czar Ferdinand of Bulgaria had sided with the Germans during the war, against the sentiments of most of his people. After the war, he had been exiled, and his son Boris had succeeded to the throne. A general election had given a majority to the Austrian Party, which was leftist, though not communist, and the president of that party, Stambolisky, headed the government. To add to its troubles, the country was regarded by the Allies as a former enemy.

With help from the Allies, General Wrangel had persuaded Stambolisky, heading the new government, to allow refuge to some of the exiled survivors of his White Army. But it was not sitting well with Stambolisky. These foreign soldiers, with rightist political attitudes, could well side with his opposition and assist in a coup d'etat. And the Soviet Union was unhappy with him for granting asylum to its mortal enemies. But the White Russian Army and its leaders were scrupulously neutral regarding Bulgaria's internal affairs. Their dreams of returning to Russia had been encouraged by the mutiny of the sailors at Kronstadt against the Bolsheviks, and incidents of fierce partisan resistance in the Caucasus.

I was still bewildered by Pokrovsky's summons. I was very young and much too junior to be any help to him. But after a splendid dinner he handed me a hundred dollars and told me to go to a certain address in Burgas and wait for him there. "I will tell you there what I want you to do."

I told him good-bye, and by the next evening I was in Burgas, the large Bulgarian port on the Black Sea. The address the general had given me was a large building on the outskirts, surrounded by a high stone wall. It had been rented by a Russian colonel who was living there and posing as a businessman organizing a small commercial fishing company. A large vessel from Constantinople was sitting in the harbor.

The ship was commanded by a Greek captain who was originally from Kertch in the Crimea. The crew of six were all from Odessa and had been longtime volunteers in the White Army. The ship was to land supplies for the partisans on the shore of the Black Sea. At first, I thought this was the mission the colonel had in mind for me. I knew that part of the world and my name was well known to the Cossacks who were resisting the Reds there. I would have accepted such an assignment in spite of the dangers; besides any patriotic motives, it would have given me a chance to look for my mother and maybe to bring her back to Bulgaria. This was not what the general had in mind. General Pokrovsky, now Captain Ivanov, arrived one night soon, accompanied by his orderly, a Cossack noncommissioned officer who was utterly devoted to him. There was a lieutenant colonel in the house who also lived under a false name. General Pokrovsky said, "Now, gentlemen, let us talk about serious matters." And, turning to me, "I have summoned you, *molodoi*, for two reasons. First of all, you come from an excellent family, renowned for its honor and its sense of loyalty. I remember your grandfather, who served three emperors without the slightest fault, and who was a hero of the war of 1877. I also knew your uncle, the colonel of the Imperial Guard, and I have had the honor of being his commanding officer. I know also that several members of your family have been killed by the Reds. Not long ago you lost your younger brother. You yourself have served under me, and even if your inexperience has caused you to make a few mistakes, I know you to be courageous and trustworthy. The second reason has precisely to do with your youth and physical strength. You will need both."

The general then told me the rest. When Denikine had finally realized that victory was hopeless, he had named Pokrovsky director of the military affairs behind the lines. In this position he had been charged with gathering all the deposits of both State and private banks, as well as the contents of private estates whose owners were assumed dead or in flight. The money was intended to support sabotage and intrigue against the Reds. He had hidden everything he had got hold of in a secret place known only to two or three people. We sat at the table listening as the general paced the room and spoke in nervous bursts.

"According to what I have learned from our Bulgarian friends, Stambolisky's police are planning an action against me. There is a traitor among us who has denounced us as an organization that intends to continue the resistance against the Reds. The Bulgarian government is friendly to the Soviet Union and is under severe pressure from them for having even admitted us. It is urgent that we hide our treasure in an absolutely secure place. It is well hidden now, but not safe enough. A really good search might uncover it, and that would mean the end of our cause. We must decide where and how to hide it better."

He turned to the two colonels and the lieutenant colonel. "I have asked you, gentlemen, to give me your suggestions on how to find another hiding place. What have you to say?"

The lieutenant colonel answered. "Excellency, the colonel and I have given it a great deal of thought. I have personally explored the territory around the city for about fifty miles. I believe the only really safe hiding place must be away from the city, in a heavily wooded area, and I think I have found the spot. It will take a tremendous amount of work. Fortunately, we have our young comrade with us now, but I wonder if even he can manage."

"I can assure you," I responded grandly, "that nothing will be too much."

"Very well, *molodoi*," said the general. "I am counting on you."

All night we discussed the project. The lieutenant colonel and I would look over the location the next day. Then the general led us downstairs into the cellar. The lieutenant colonel removed about twenty bricks from one of the walls. They were so well matched to the rest of the wall that it would have been impossible to find the hiding place without tearing the whole cellar apart. I could see only part of the treasure but what I did see amazed me: foreign currency, bushel baskets of diamonds and emeralds, silver plate and gold. A fabulous treasure.

Then it dawned on me why the general had had the bricks taken off and was removing some of the treasure. He was going to take some of the money for his own needs and give each of us enough to support ourselves before the treasure was buried. Early the next morning, he bade us farewell and promised to return. We felt somehow that we would never see him again.

We had decided that we would divide the treasure four ways and bury each portion a half mile away from the other. We got right down to the task of exploring the forest for hiding places where we could work without being noticed. We roamed all day without seeing a soul within a radius of six or seven miles. Still, we planned to work only at night and search for our hiding spots during the day.

The lieutenant colonel went off in search of some cases

Nicholas Svidine as the director of the Cossacks of Kuban. *Collection of the Author*.

Above   Svidine's grandfather (left) in 1895. *Collection of the Author.*

Below   In front of the palace of Czarskoie Selo, at the celebration of the centennial of the regiment of the Czar's guards. Svidine's grandfather (with a full white beard) is to the right of the Czar in the second row. *Collection of the Author.*

Above Officers of the Czar's personal guard. Svidine's uncle is indicated with an X. *Collection of the Author.*

Below The Czar and the royal family in the garden of the palace of Czarskoie Selo with officers from his personal guard. *Roger Viollet.*

Svidine's grandfather (left in the photograph above) and his uncle (below, indicated with an X) on their property. *Collection of the Author.*

The Great War followed by the Revolution and then the Civil War. Nicholas Svidine remained loyal to the Czar and served in the White Army. *Above*, Svidine with the artillery of General Wrangel's White Army. *Roger Viollet and A.P.N.*

Nicholas Svidine with the Cossacks of Kuban (Svidine is indicated with an X). *Collection of the Author.*

Above   En route to the treasure.

Opposite   Nicholas Svidine (right) in Constantinople. *Collection of the Author.*

Nicholas Svidine in 1939
(above) and today
(below). *Collection of the
Author.*

the Russian army had used to store rifle cartridges. And I was sent to find some waxed paper we could wrap the currency and stock certificates in to keep them dry. I had to go to Sofia. I thought from there I might get a letter to my mother. I was worried sick about her; most of my relatives were either dead or in prison. It was very complicated to get a letter from Bulgaria into Russia. Germany was the only country that had postal relations with Russia, so one had to send a letter to Germany with a request to the postal authorities there to forward it to Russia. Along with my letter I sent a return envelope marked to myself, "General Delivery, Sofia."

When I got back, the lieutenant colonel and I got to work. The treasure had been brought out of Russia in six or seven large zinc cases. It was only when I was helping the lieutenant colonel divide it up to put it into smaller cases that I got any real idea of how large it was. In spite of my youth and inexperience, even I could see that it was worth a fabulous sum. I have forgotten what figure the colonel cited, but I know that it turned my head. I still remember, fifty years later, how awed I was.

One case contained thousands of gold rubles and presented us with a terrible problem, since we had only about twenty smaller cases and the original containers were too large to hide. Finally, we bought two medium-sized iron water tanks for the gold pieces, but we had to lug them into the forest empty, then bring the gold pieces out in sacks and fill them. We later buried these in the third and fourth hiding places. We had a terrible time, as well, with about four hundred and fifty pounds of platinum — the purest in the world, the colonel assured me — but at least it was molded in flat bars and didn't take up as much room as the gold pieces. We wrapped the platinum bars in heavy rags and put them inside burlap bags and then wrapped the whole thing in big leather pouches. These were to go into the first and second hiding places. Another large part of the treasure was made up of about forty-five pounds of jewelry set with precious stones, diamonds, emeralds, and rubies. Some of the stones were huge and must have represented large fortunes just by themselves. There were some smaller bags with pounds of loose, uncut precious stones of various sizes. Then there were a number of wooden boxes literally stuffed with foreign notes and currency, most of them English pounds. The stock and bond certificates were interesting because they represented some of the greatest companies in the world. I remember there were some from de Beers diamonds, and from the Canadian Pacific railroad. Besides the valuables, one case contained documents which, General Pokrovsky told me, would be enormously important for future historians. The band the documents were tied with was inscribed in red, in Russian: "Top secret. Of the greatest importance to the State." I can still see the inscription as if it were before my very eyes. How would I evaluate the treasure as a whole? It's hard to give even an approximation. But I would estimate that it was worth over a hundred million dollars.

Our first expedition took place a few days after I got back. We set out early in the evening, since the first spot we had picked was a very long way. We had hidden our tools there. I had bought three powerful flashlights in Sofia. It was exhausting work. The lieutenant colonel was an old man and had a heart condition. The ground was frozen and we had to dig a deep hole at least three and a half feet. It was summer and so daybreak came just as we had gotten the cases in place. We filled the hole in, camouflaged it and hid our tools, and then walked a half mile. At that point we fell on the ground and slept all through the afternoon. Afterward, we waited for dusk before we dared return to the house.

The following night, on our second expedition, we had a bad scare. We had just begun to dig when the lieutenant colonel suggested that we stop and eat something. We were leaning against a tree, relaxing, when we heard footsteps about a hundred yards away, then voices that were not speaking Bulgarian. I recognized it as Turkish because it resembled Tartar, which some of our servants had spoken.

We drew our pistols — we had been ordered to kill anyone who came upon us and to conceal their bodies.

Whoever they were, they halted and remained there, in silence, for almost an hour. We thought there were five or six of them. Finally, they moved away, in the same direction from which they had come, toward the sea.

When we had finished our work we went to examine the spot where they had remained for so long. It was light, and after searching for a bit, we found a natural excavation hidden under a thicket. Inside it was all kinds of foreign merchandise. Our visitors had apparently been

Turkish smugglers who were delivering their goods to their Bulgarian connections.

Our discovery could have had serious consequences. We had chosen their hiding place as a site to bury part of our treasure. If the smugglers had come upon us, we would have had no choice but to fire. Given the numbers involved, there would have been some doubt as to the outcome.

But the rest of our work proceeded smoothly, and we were relieved when it was over. Our main concern was the colonel, who was having a great deal of trouble with his heart. After our work was finished, he admitted that he had had several attacks. There was no way to get any medicine for him.

It was now a full month since I had mailed the letter to my mother and I was impatient to get to the post office in Sofia even though I could hardly expect a response so soon. Nonetheless, as soon as I arrived in Sofia I went there and, with great apprehension, inquired at the general delivery window. I almost fainted with emotion when the clerk handed me the envelope I had addressed to myself a month before. I walked out of the post office, feeling almost drunk, and sat down on a bench before the magnificent cathedral of Alexander Nevsky.

I saw a tiny bit of paper and unfamiliar writing and knew that my fears had been justified. "Dear Nicholas," the letter read, "I am a Cossack who used to work in your home. When your letter arrived, they tacked it up on the bulletin board in the meeting room of our soviet. I am terribly sorry to have to tell you that your mother died on

April 21 last year of typhus. I hope you are well." My mother was forty years old. I walked around for several hours and then returned to Burgas. The two colonels tried their best to console me. To pass the time, the lieutenant colonel and I had gotten into the habit of going to a café frequented by Russians, where we played chess. We met a young Bulgarian who was employed in the police headquarters and who, like the majority of Bulgarians, was a Russophil and disliked the present government.

One evening, quite late, we had just finished our chess game. He walked in and stood facing me and with a movement of his head suggested that we two step outside. I followed casually. He was waiting for me behind a tree. "You must leave immediately," he said in Russian. "A few minutes ago I received a telegram for the prefect from Sofia. It contains three names: yours, the colonel's and the lieutenant colonel's. The prefect is ordered to arrest you immediately and send you to Sofia under heavy guard until the authorities arrive from the capital. You must hurry. I have to deliver the message immediately."

"Thank you, my friend," I said. 'Tell me how much time we have to collect the colonel and a few things."

"At most a half hour," he replied. "And don't forget that the prefect has a car."

We shook hands, and I went in to get my friend. I asked him to follow me without wasting a moment and on the way to the house I explained what was happening. He was worried about the colonel. "He is old and sick; we cannot leave him alone here. What are we going to do?"

When we got there, we told the colonel what was going

on and asked him to get ready as fast as possible and to gather any compromising papers. As he was getting the papers together, he clasped his hand to his heart and lay down on his bed. "It is nothing," he said. "It will pass." And with that he closed his eyes and died. "He is better off," my friend said. "He could never have stood what is ahead of us."

We kissed him, and recited a prayer for the repose of his soul. Then we took our handguns and the money and papers and left. The closest border we could head for was the Turkish. To avoid the police, we circled the city. In the distance, we could hear the siren of the prefect's auto.

It was a dark, warm night and we made good time. As we walked along we tore up the papers we had taken with us. The area between Burgas and the border was sparsely populated and heavily wooded. It was a simple matter to avoid the few villages.

When day broke, we found a well-covered hiding spot in a grove and slept there for several hours. When we awoke, we were dying of hunger and thirst. A little way along we came to a large farm. The lieutenant colonel guarded our arsenal while I went to get something to eat and drink. I had a heavy walking stick with me, luckily, because no sooner had I entered the yard than I was attacked by a half-dozen savage dogs. They had me backed up against a wall when an old woman appeared from the house. She chased the dogs away, yelling at them and throwing stones.

She lived alone in the house with her young grandson. I explained to her that I was Russian and that my friend and I were looking for work in the forests. I showed her my money and asked her if I could buy something to eat. She sold me some bread, two dozen eggs, a wheel of cheese and a large jug of milk. That was fine, but how was I to get out by the dogs? The old woman worked out a stratagem, coaxing them into the stable with some cheese. While they were fighting over it, she closed the door and I got away.

As day broke on the third day, we saw a barrack with the Bulgarian flag in the distance. This was the border. We moved off the road and waited until dark to try to pass over. It was very hot, but we found a small stream where we could drink and wash ourselves. The day dragged on and we got increasingly nervous. Greek troops were guarding the border, since all of what had been European Turkey was occupied by the Allies. At last, night came and we moved out slowly. We clambered into a stream, but there was no way of knowing in the dark when we had crossed over to the "other side."

The night was completely still. We would have prayed to heaven for some wind or rain, even a storm, rather than that quiet in which our every step resounded. We held our pistols ready and agreed that we would not fall alive into the hands of the border patrols. We walked for about another twenty minutes, about ten yards away from each other. I was just about to say to my companion that we had probably crossed the border when we heard a shout fifty yards behind us, "*Stoi!*" — "Halt" — in Bulgarian. We were still not across.

A hundred yards ahead lay the shadowy outline of the forest, and bullets whistled around us. One passed so close to my right ear that I was briefly deafened. One more burst of energy and we reached cover. Bullets struck the tree trunks. We were so out of breath and tired that we couldn't run any more. Our only recourse was to resist, to return fire until we had recovered enough strength to move on. The lieutenant colonel took cover behind a thick tree trunk, and I lay down behind a felled tree.

Immediately another foe appeared — a Greek patrol drawn by the sound of the Bulgarian firing. They could not see what was going on and began firing back at the Bulgarians. They soon saw their mistake and began firing in our direction. They could not see us, but from the echo of the bullets as they hit the tree trunks, we knew they were both in front and behind us. We were in a cross fire. Without a word between us, my companion turned his fire on the Greeks, who were nearer to him, while I aimed at the Bulgarians. We had semiautomatic weapons and we fired in short bursts to conserve our ammunition. Off and on we would hear cries of wounded men. We were in a much better position: invisible in the shade of the forest, while we could spot their patrols against the horizon as the sky grew lighter.

I held off their advance by hitting three of the five men who remained able to fight. Nonetheless, our situation was worsening. The patrols would certainly be reinforced, and our ammunition was running out. I had only two charges left. I was dashing to my companion when I heard his firing stop. I reached him crawling on my hands and knees, but he was dead, a bullet in his head.

I could still hear firing behind me but the bullets were no longer whistling by. I then took my friend's ammunition, money and papers, fired another round, and took off through the underbrush. The forest was not very dense, and soon I was able to stand up and run at full speed.

9

At Loose Ends in Turkey

SINCE I HAD had some rest during the shooting match, I set out on an all-day, all-night marathon. Though I stopped from time to time, I was utterly exhausted by the end, too tired even to feel hungry. My mouth was so dry I could hardly swallow. As I stood at the edge of a small wood at dawn I could hear dogs barking in the distance and headed in that direction.

I was moving along cautiously when I saw a man watching me from behind a bush. I took out my Mauser. He called out *"kardache,"* the Turkish word for friend. I had come on a *"pomak,"* one of those Bulgarians who had been converted to Islam by the Turks. We spoke to each other in Bulgarian. I explained to him that I trying to get to Constantinople to look for work, because there was none to be found in Bulgaria, and that some Greeks had fired on me as I was crossing the frontier and I had returned their fire. He replied that he hated the Greek dogs and would help me as much as he could. He offered me food, though all I wanted was something to drink and some sleep.

He led me to a small thatched log cabin. He took care of about two hundred sheep that belonged to him and his family and hated the Greek soldiers, who were constantly stealing them. There was a huge jug of cool, clear spring water. He smiled at me as I gulped it down. Then he piled some sheepskins in the corner and I threw myself on them. The shepherd covered me with skins until I was completely hidden. I had my arms ready to defend myself in the event of danger. I might be discovered at any moment by a Greek search party, or the shepherd might betray me. He had an honest face — and guests are sacred in his country — but I couldn't know what was going on inside his head.

I fell asleep immediately and when I awoke, it was night. I had slept away the entire day. The shepherd was sitting on a stool near the doorway and when he saw me emerge from the sheepskins, he smiled and wished me a good evening.

"The Greeks were here looking for you. You and your friend killed a lot of them, and some Bulgarians, too. They looked in here but didn't see anything. They told me I would get a reward if I saw you and reported your whereabouts to the police. I gave them a lamb to get rid of them." I was ashamed that I had doubted his goodwill. I shook his hand warmly and thanked him.

I felt strong again and hungry enough to eat a sheep. My host gave me an enormous piece of cold mutton and some homemade cheese, which I washed down with spring water, since wine is forbidden to Moslems. As I ate, my new friend counseled me on how to avoid all the traps on the way to Constantinople. The most dangerous places, he said, were on the outskirts. They were occupied by French, English and Italian soldiers, who patrolled all the roads leading into the city. I might be arrested and thrown into prison for entering Turkey illegally. Not to mention the gunfight at the border — the Greeks had better not learn that I had taken part in that battle. (There had been two Greeks killed and three wounded, and the Bulgarians had one dead and five wounded, as I later learned.)

I had to get moving. The Greeks might come back at any time. One last time I thanked my Bulgarian friend and gave him my automatic pistol. Tears came to his eyes. I couldn't have kept it anyhow. It was too heavy and hard to hide, not to speak of incriminating. I cautioned him that it could get him into serious trouble and warned him to keep it hidden.

I practically had to lose my temper in order to get him to accept twenty English pounds, a small fortune to him. Furnished with a supply of meat, bread and cheese, I set out at about 10 P.M.

I moved along a narrow path, my Mauser in my hand, a bullet in the chamber. It was a clear night. The clouds had disappeared and the landscape was brightly lit by a half moon. Suddenly, two uniformed figures loomed in front of me, Greek policemen. But they had made a bad mistake. Instead of carrying their carbines at the ready, they had them slung over their shoulders. I didn't want to kill them but I had to do something. I fired at their legs and they crumpled with screams of pain.

I ran most of the night, then slept for a couple of hours in a thicket, ate something, and started out again, avoiding the villages. From the top of a hill I saw a Greek patrol in the distance.

At dusk I came on a small stream and decided to spend the night there. My feet were killing me. I bathed them in the stream for a long time and rubbed them with grease from the mutton. I found a sheltered spot and spent a peaceful night, and in the morning I felt refreshed and ready for the road. That day passed without incident. But my shoes were falling apart, which was a serious problem. The ground was rocky and in a day or two I would be barefoot.

I spent the next night near a stream and in the morning I decided to risk everything. I had to find a hamlet where I wouldn't be discovered by the police but where I could buy a pair of the woven shoes the peasants wear, which are comfortable for walking in the mountains and forests. In the afternoon, I spotted a tiny hamlet, just a few houses around a small mosque. I had no choice but to dare it since I also needed more provisions.

As I entered the village a pack of dogs set up a terrible racket and some Turks came out of their houses. I greeted them with *"Shalom alechem"* the common greeting in all Moslem countries. They began to speak to me in Turkish but I indicated by sign language that I didn't understand. They were neither hostile nor friendly — merely suspicious. They exchanged anxious glances and asked if I were Greek, English or French. I told the truth: "I am *ourousse* [Russian]."

To my great surprise, their attitude immediately changed. They began shaking my hands and slapping me on the back. One of them led me by the hand into his house. Then I grasped the reason for their change of heart. My Turkish host kept repeating over and over "Kemal Pasha [Ataturk], *ourous kardache!*" Kemal Pasha was battling the Greek army in Asia Minor with arms supplied by the Soviet Union. The Turks did not make any distinction between Red and White Russians. All Russians were "*kardaches*" to them.

A crowd gathered around me while I ate. I explained that I was trying to get to Istanbul (the Turks disliked the name Constantinople), showed them my tattered shoes and a five-dollar bill. (The rest of the money was tied around my waist in a cloth belt.) No one would take my money but in a few minutes they had set before me several pairs of boots of the kind worn by Balkan peasants, made of strips of sheepskin. They are so light you hardly know you have them on. One wears them with long woolen stockings the women weave, and a pair of these were brought to me. Then I was escorted to the fountain in the courtyard of the mosque, where I washed my feet, put on the stockings and my size 44 shoes, and felt like a new man.

I spent the night in this hospitable village. All evening long I heard patriotic songs in which I could distinguish only one word: Kemal Pasha. The Turks were incredibly proud of his victories over the Greeks. On the other hand, they detested the Allies, who occupied their capital, and explained to me in sign language that it would not take their hero long to throw them out.

The next day the entire village accompanied me to the Istanbul road. On my back was another gift from these Turkish peasants, a large embroidered cloth bag full of provisions. Once again, they adamantly refused any payment. As I walked along I thought of the wonderful people I had met since crossing the Bulgarian border and of the age-old traditions that make a stranger a cherished friend to them.

Of course, the Turks knew nothing of my adventures with the patrols and I had no way of explaining, as they pointed out the road to Istanbul, that I had to avoid the direct routes. So after a few kilometers I struck off on a path that ran parallel to the road and two days later I sighted Constantinople. Night was falling as I arrived at Galata, an outlying district of the city on the Bosporus. I was glad it was dark, as I was filthy and my clothes were torn and unkempt. While I walked through more and more densely populated neighborhoods, people stared at my strange getup and I grew more and more dismayed. As I turned a corner, I saw two men whose clothes identified them as Russian soldiers. I asked if they could tell me where I could spend the night.

We were standing under a streetlight. One of them looked at my costume and said, "Where have you come from in that condition?"

"I walked all the way from Bulgaria. Tomorrow I will go to see our military attaché."

"Are you an officer?"

"Yes."

"Then maybe you're part of this Bulgarian business that everyone's talking about."

"I don't know what you're talking about. I fled from Bulgaria to escape being arrested."

"Very interesting. We are a Russian naval and a merchant marine officer and we live in a rented house a few steps away. Come and tell us your tale and let's see what we can do for you."

My appearance caused a sensation among my clean, well-dressed hosts. "Where did you find that ragamuffin?" one of them asked the officer who led me in.

They all laughed. But they stopped laughing when they heard where I had come from and why. Everyone crowded around to listen. Someone showed me to the shower they had built for themselves, and each one brought me a piece of clothing from his modest wardrobe — one, trousers, another underwear, a shirt, and so on. When I had shaved and looked human again, I sat down at the table and told them the whole story, except the part about the treasure.

They, in turn, filled me in on what had happened after the defeat at Burgas. The newspapers had been full of it. Stambolisky had turned against our organization in Bulgaria, which had wanted to continue the fight against the Bolsheviks by any and all means. Colonel Samokhvalov, our chief of staff in Sofia, had been arrested and imprisoned. The membership roll of the secret organization was found in his desk. Except for the colonel and myself, who had been alerted in time, everyone had been arrested. General Pokrovsky had been killed by the police during arrest and General Koutiepov, commander-in-chief of the Russian troops in Bulgaria, had been expelled.

So, General Pokrovsky, the colonel, and the lieutenant colonel were the treasure's first victims. There would be others. I was so upset that I couldn't sleep in spite of my exhaustion. I was the sole survivor among those who knew about the treasure. What made it all the more strange was that I had learned of its existence only recently, and that those who had gathered it were all dead. I was overwhelmed by the responsibility.

Should I speak to the highest ranking Russian military authorities? The three of us had solemnly sworn to General Pokrovsky not to reveal anything without his explicit permission. But now the general was dead and my promise had no more force. Whom should I tell? Considering the moral standard of our high-ranking officers — with the exception of Denikine and Wrangel — the treasure would certainly be misappropriated in short order. By the next morning I had made a decision to speak of the treasure to no one for the time being. It was securely hidden, though I had no way of recovering it. Later I would confide in someone I trusted absolutely.

I had breakfast with the officers, borrowed a little Turkish money, and promised to return in the evening. I set off downtown. The first thing I had to do was change some money to buy some clothes. At Galata I found a Greek money changer and changed fifty English pounds, quite a large sum for the times.

All the foreign diplomatic missions were still function-
ing in Constantinople. The Russian military attaché was
quite helpful when he'd heard my story. On the spot, he
provided me with identity papers, in Russian and French,
under the name of Sergei Orel, as he thought it would be
safer not to use my real name until public interest in the
Sofia affair died down. He asked me whether I had any
money. I was faced with a dilemma. If I said yes, it would
seem strange, given the general poverty of the Russian
refugees. On the other hand, I knew he couldn't be very
well off and it embarrassed me to take money I didn't
need. I replied that two or three Turkish pounds would do
me for the moment. He seemed relieved and added, since
I had told him I had borrowed the clothes I was wearing,
"I'll give you a letter to Mme. Ilovaiskaia, the general's
daughter, who is secretary to Miss Mitchell, the head of
the American Red Cross. She will outfit you from head to
toe."

I thanked the general sincerely and promised to let him
know my address as soon as I had found somewhere to
live. At the headquarters of the American Red Cross,
Mme. Ilovaiskaia provided me with a fine blue pinstripe
suit (with a label from a Philadelphia tailor), shirts and
underwear, shoes, and even a hat.

A month later, I received a visit at my small hotel in
Galata from an officer who served the military attaché.
His superior wanted to see me as soon as possible. The
next morning, when I went to the embassy, the general
received me promptly. He led me into a private office and

closed the door carefully. His first question took me off guard.

"What do you know of the treasure General Pokrovsky was guarding?"

"What treasure, Excellency?"

"You know nothing of it?"

"I only met General Pokrovsky, under whom I had served in Russia, two months before I fled Bulgaria. The general never spoke to me of any treasure. I have no idea whether such a thing exists."

"In that case, *essaoul*, let me ask you where you got the money you have been spending. You told me you had no money and I lent you five Turkish pounds. Now you are living in a hotel that, modest as it is, costs a pound a day. You eat in a restaurant every day that must cost another pound. You bought a suit from an Armenian tailor. Over and above this, I know that you have given over one hundred Turkish pounds to various refugees. Allow me to ask you where this money — a small fortune for a refugee — comes from."

They've been watching me ever since I got to Constantinople, I said to myself. If only I had told him that General Pokrovsky had given each of his aides a small amount. Too late now. "It is true, Excellency, that I had no money when I arrived. What I did not say — and I don't know why I should have —is that I brought a few valuables from Russia, including a heavy gold cigarette box signed by Fabergé. It was a family heirloom and I didn't want to sell it but as you know, there is no work here and I was forced to." (In fact, I had sold it in Yugoslavia.)

"In that case, you can tell me to whom you sold it."

"To an American tourist on the *Mauritania*. I didn't want to sell it in a jewelry shop. They're all run by Greeks and Armenians. You know what a ridiculous price they would have given me."

He was looking me in the eye and I stared back. Then he asked me to let him know where I could be reached if I left the hotel, but I never saw him again.

I stayed at the hotel two more months, until my money ran out, and then I moved into a boardinghouse for refugees where it was only five piasters for a bed for the night. It was a wooden building and, like many Turkish houses, harbored a fantastic colony of bedbugs that were impossible to get rid of. The only solution would have been to burn the whole thing down, bedbugs and all. The beds were made of iron and we burned out every possible hiding place on them with gasoline. Then we set the legs in tin cans of gasoline but the damned bugs crawled up to the ceiling and dropped down on us while we slept. Sometimes, when I was half crazy with them, I would take my bedclothes and sleep on the lawn of one of the abandoned cemeteries in the city.

Then the day arrived when I didn't even have the five piasters. It was winter, an unpleasant season in Constantinople, with icy winds and rain almost every day. I was facing disaster and had nowhere to turn. Once more, good luck intervened. On the main street of Pera I saw someone who looked familiar. We gazed at each other and then we fell into each other's arms. It was like a miracle. At the military school at Irkutsk, my bunk and Teliatnikov's had been next to each other. He was from Tashkent, had been an assistant manager of a bank, and was forty years old; I was then just eighteen. Now he told me of how he had escaped from Russia through Vladivostok, had roamed over half the world and ended up in Constantinople. For two years now he had been the chief accountant at the Nobel Company, the principal owner of the Baku oil fields. The Bolsheviks were selling Nobel his own oil. My friend thought it couldn't last because the communists needed the oil badly themselves and were only selling it for foreign credits. He loaned me a little money and promised to try to help. Two days later he arranged for me to come to work for Nobel as a gasoline salesman.

So there I was, with a Crimean Tartar driver who spoke Turkish. Every day we went to a different neighborhood in a specially equipped wagon drawn by two mules carrying twenty- and fifty-liter cans. Most often I had to carry them on my shoulders because the streets were too narrow or too steep for the wagon. The driver helped me but it was still very hard work. I stank so of gas that people turned away as I passed. I had to sleep in the stable with the mules but I got pretty good pay, ate three meals a day, and my compatriots envied me my job. Twice a week it brought me to the rear of the famous Pera Palace Hotel, where I gazed at the lovely women on the arms of the Allied officers. The Italian officers, with the comic opera uniforms, were the most elegant.

I still did not know what to do about the treasure — whether I should abandon it forever or tell the right person. Who was the right person?

I worked at Nobel for four months and got to know

Constantinople as few foreigners do. I also learned to speak Turkish in order to bargain with the grocers. But when Nobel stopped buying oil, I was out of work again.

After a few days of near panic, I heard that the English army was hiring Russian refugees to work on their bases in the Dardanelles. I had no idea what kind of work it was but I had no choice so I signed on for a year. A boat took us to an English base on the right bank of the straits facing Chanak, where we were lodged in unheated Turkish army barracks. We slept on the bare wooden floor and shivered with cold day and night. It rained all the time and the wind was freezing. We could never get our clothing dry. Canned meat and soup were the only hot food we had and so we were perpetually hungry. We used to steal a few cartons of food once in a while but eventually we stopped as a point of honor. We worked hard and long in the rain and mud. The English noncoms treated us like prisoners even though we were free workers. A lot of the time, we worked unloading heavy cases of shells. I wondered why the British were stockpiling so much military material when their war was over. Kemal Pasha was continuing his successful campaign against the Greeks but the English had remained neutral in that conflict.

About a month after I arrived, we were ordered to unload cases of heavy artillery shells. Four men could hardly lift the cases. Since I spoke English, my comrades designated me to inform the sergeant that we could not and would not. The cases were unwieldy and if one fell, we would be blown to bits. The sergeant was well aware of this and kept his distance. I approached him, but instead of listening to our complaint, he started to curse at me as only an English sergeant can. "You have no right to insult me," I said. "I am not a prisoner or a slave."

He went wild, and dragged me by the arm to the major in charge. I took off my cap. The major put his on. He sentenced me to a hundred and sixty-eight hours (why a hundred and sixty-eight hours instead of a week?) in prison for disobedience. I was not permitted to utter one word. They locked me in a barbed wire enclosure with two tents where there were three other Russians, who were being punished for refusing to eat corned beef every day.

It was the first time I had ever been locked up. At the crack of dawn we were rousted out with yelling and swearing. All day, with only a short break for lunch, we were made to run on the double to the beach, fill a fifty-kilo bag with sand, run back to the prison with it, and empty it onto a pile. When the pile was large enough, we took the sand back bag by bag to where we'd gotten it. When we slowed down, the English soldiers threatened us with long clubs.

One night after it had rained for twenty-four hours the tents were flooded up to our knees. We complained to the guards but all they would allow us to do was fill some sacks with sand and pile them up so we could squat on them. We were trembling with the cold, our teeth chattering so that we could barely talk.

The next day I told my companion, a sublieutenant, that I had decided to break out and that he was welcome to come with me. He agreed. I had noticed that by lifting the barbed wire where we gathered the sand you could dig a ditch deep enough to slip under. The next night the rain stopped but there came a very strong wind, almost of hurricane force. Our tents were almost blown away but fortunately it was a dark, starless night. We waited until very late and then slipped out of the tent. We filled some sacks with damp sand and slipped them one by one under the wire. This opened up a narrow passageway. It took a long time and we were very nervous. The guards, who slept in a small wooden barracks at the far end of the compound, could emerge at any moment and they would almost certainly shoot us. Our hands were bleeding from the barbed wire. My companion was smaller than I and slipped out easily. I had some trouble but I finally managed to squeeze through.

We took the road that ran along the strait to Gallipoli. Late in the morning, when were some distance from the camp, my companion suddenly shouted, "Watch out. They're after us." Sure enough, there were two British soldiers on bicycles with dogs about a kilometer away and moving toward us.

There was nowhere to retreat to. On the right was the water, and on the left a steep rise covered with thick underbrush. Ahead about three hundred yards away there was a small bay, where four men were unloading stone blocks onto the bank. Without stopping to think, we dashed toward them. They were Turks. I explained that the English were after us because we didn't want to work for them and as soon as they heard the magic word *ourousse* they said, "Jump into the felucca."

When the English soldiers got there five minutes later, we were one hundred yards from the shore. The dogs were barking angrily at having lost their trail and the English soldiers concluded that we must be underwater. They waited around for an hour or two before returning to base. In the evening, the Turks reentered the cove. It was too late to work so they dropped anchor about fifty meters from shore and invited us to spend the night. We accepted gratefully. They gave us tincture of iodine for our hands and a meal of grilled fish and sour milk. Our hosts began to sing and again, over and over, we heard the name Kemal Pasha. The night passed uneventfully and early the next morning, we thanked our rescuers and pressed on to Gallipoli.

The appearance of the city, which was empty and abandoned, was sinister. It was bizarre to see a good-sized city inhabited by nothing but wild cats, who would run when we approached, and by pigs darting in every direction. Finally we found a few French soldiers who were guarding the lighthouse, and four Russians — the sole survivors of General Koutiepov's army, which had been evacuated into Bulgaria and Yugoslavia. A single trace of their encampment remained — a pyramid of stones. Every soldier and officer had brought one stone to build it, the inscription read. This moving monument was all that testified to the fate of an "army of chevaliers," as one French writer called it.

The Russians told us that the Greek population had abandoned the city when Kemal Pasha's army reached the opposite shore of the Sea of Marmara. It was better to be a refugee in Greece than face the Turkish soldiers, who did not treat Greeks gently.

When I got back to Constantinople, I faced the same problems as before: I was a penniless refugee in a city where there was no work to be found. There was a three- or four-month waiting list to emigrate to America and even then I would have had to have at least twenty-five Turkish pounds, which I had no way of getting.

Once again, a solution presented itself — to enlist in the Foreign Legion. My companion and I went to the recruitment office and were interviewed by a French officer. "Formal swearing in," he informed us "will take place at Fort Saint-Jean in Marseilles. In the meantime, you will be lodged and fed at the post here."

He gave us a note for the commanding officer. The post was a formidable building surrounded by high walls that looked more like a prison than an army camp. We arrived at mealtime, and for the first time in three days ate all we wanted. It wasn't very good, but as the saying goes, we didn't look a gift horse in the mouth. However, we realized immediately that we were trapped. Once inside there was no getting out. The next day, a transport ship arrived from Marseilles. Some legionnaires who were being demobilized for illness or wounds stopped at the post on their way back home. There were Serbs, Bulgarians, and Rumanians. Needless to say, we asked them about life in the legion.

Their response was unanimous: "The legion is living hell. You work on the roads twelve hours a day in the broiling sun. At night, as often as not, you have to fight, since Morocco is in open revolt. The discipline is cruel and punishment is brutal. The only relief, when you get your lousy pay, is to get drunk enough to forget."

All we could think of was to escape. In two days the transport would leave for Marseilles and formal enlistment, which would mean five years of hell. But we didn't know how escape would be possible. We had noticed that certain trusties went out in the evening, and there were also some civilian employees, mostly Greeks, who left for the night. They had to show their exit permits to a noncommissioned officer. On alternate days, the officer in charge was a Sengalese who did not even read the papers, just waved the men on. My comrade and I did have Russian military identity papers. We waited for the Sengalese noncom to come on duty and got in line. We flashed our papers at him and he let us pass. Once outside, we ran as fast as we could.

The next day I remembered that the owner of the Russian newspaper in Constantinople, a man named Maximov, had known my father. I went to ask him for work. By chance, the man who had distributed the papers to the retail dealers had just left for America, so I inherited his menial job. It paid just enough to feed me and allow me to feed my blood to the bedbugs that infested the quarters reserved for Russian refugees. I couldn't go on like this. I had to find a way to get out.

One day I read in one of the newspapers I distributed that a ship headed for Marseilles with a French regiment would also take Russian refugees who had French visas. I was off that day, so I went up to the Galata port. Maybe I would have a chance to say good-bye to someone I knew. And I did meet a lieutenant I had known. He had studied at the conservatory and now led a Russian orchestra and had a three-month engagement in a nightclub in 'Nice. Out of the blue, he said: "Do you want to go to France?"

"Of course. What a question! But how? I have no money and no visa."

"But it's very simple, my friend. Get your bags, get on board, and I'll tell the boarding officer that your name is on the group passport."

I ran home, grabbed my two bags, ran back and up the long gangplank right into the arms of the boarding officer "Passport?" he asked. From below the orchestra leader yelled up, "He's with us. His name is on the group passport."

After a bit he came on board and hid me with their baggage. I waited there for six or seven hours, scared to death. Then I heard the most beautiful sound imaginable, the ship's whistle; we were under way. Eventually, my friend came to rescue me. "You can come out now. Even if they find you out, there's nothing they can do. You're on your way to Marseilles."

The crossing took five days. The French soldiers fed me from their rations.

10

France in the Twenties

SO, FOR THE FOURTH TIME, I was fleeing, leaving behind what little I possessed. What would become of me in Marseilles? The thought tormented me. But when we arrived, it turned out that there were about twenty of my compatriots on board in the same fix I was in, with no passport or visas. "These damned Russians," the commissioner of the port police said with a tolerant smile, "they keep arriving from all sides." They let us in and ordered us to go to the Russian consulate to get proper papers and then to report to the local employment office.

It was September 24, 1923. Everything was odd in this land of my dreams that I now saw for the first time . . . both strange and enchanting. After four years of nightmare, the French were living life to the hilt. There was a lot of construction and workers were needed everywhere. Things were cheap and one could actually live on one's salary. In their effort to forget hardship and bereavement, the French were living as if there were no tormorrow.

All of us were offered work in the Département of the Aisne in a metal factory near Soissons, not far from Laon. We were issued tickets for the train and set out, hungry and somewhat bewildered. None of us had a penny in his pocket and we were happy just to get where we were going. Our good humor was short-lived. We disembarked, not even at a station, but at a makeshift wooden barrack. The surroundings looked like a picture of the moon — completely barren, not a tree, nothing but trenches and excavations. We asked a railroad clerk where the metal factory was. He gazed back at us with an ironic expression. "The factory? Well, you see the road that goes up the hill over there? When you reach the top, you will see your factory." He smiled. In spite of our hunger, we formed a small military detachment and marched off, singing. We got to the top of the hill. There was no factory. There were about twenty barracks and long rows of something we could not make out. (They turned out to be piles of shells and shrapnel.) A youngster came along on a bicycle and I asked where the factory was. "What factory?" he asked. I showed him the paper that had been given us in Marseilles with the name of the factory. "There is no factory here. Look at your papers. You see, it's in Alsace. All we do here is to gather the shells from the fields, defuse them, and send them to the factory."

We had been tricked once again. Now we were under contract for a year and we had been lied to about the nature of the work, and not told anything of the dangers involved. We agreed that we could not accept it and that we would announce our decision as soon as we arrived at the barracks. As we drew closer, we could see that one of the barracks flew the banner of the Red Cross. I asked to speak to whoever was in charge, and a man came out immediately to greet us. When we told him our decision, he blew up. "How dare you? Do you think I'm an idiot? You signed for a year's work, your trip was paid for, and now you refuse to work. You are asking to be put in jail. I'll telephone the police to come and arrest you."

"You are the one who should be under arrest, monsieur," I replied. "Look at my papers. It says in black and white that we are supposed to work in a metal factory. Where is the factory? We've been lied to and we're not such idiots that we're going to get killed for a few francs. There is a Red Cross barrack full of injured men. We're the ones who are going to complain."

He changed his tune. "Listen, the work really isn't dangerous and I'll raise your salary if that's the problem." We laughed at him and went off to find the mayor.

"This is not the first time," he told us, "that these people have deceived their workers. You are absolutely correct to refuse. My advice to you is to go to Laon and apply for work at the labor office."

We had eaten nothing for two days and I felt as if my legs were about to cave in. I had made friends with a lieutenant about my age and we had decided to hang in together. The others had left before us, so by the time we arrived at the employment office, they had already been hired by a threshing factory. The only jobs left were on a farm in the village of Chalandry — it was called the Château-Chalandry and was about seven miles away. We must have looked pretty sour at the prospect of such a long walk because the office manager finally asked us when we had last eaten. When he heard, he gave us some bread and butter.

We walked to the farm by fields of sugar beets. We ate one of them and felt a little better. I remember that we arrived at the farm at suppertime. We had expected something grand because it was called a "château," but it was only a mediocre farm with a silly-looking tower, from which it must have gotten its name.

The farmhouse was in the middle of a large courtyard surrounded by barns. We saw an old man, one of the owners. He ran the farm with his brother-in-law. "Do you know how to do farm work?" he asked. My companion did not speak French so I answered for both: "Yes, sir. We know all about farms. We used to be farm workers." He looked at us skeptically. "I don't really believe you were farmers, but we'll see about that." He looked over our papers and then invited us into the kitchen for something to eat. "If you work as well as you eat," he said, "I have made a good bargain."

After supper, he took us over to a ladder. "Climb up there," he told us. "There are blankets and someone will wake you in the morning."

I was so exhausted that when someone woke me up I felt as if I had slept for only an hour. After a measly breakfast, we went out to pick beets. We had arrived at the hardest work season of the year. We used huge pitchforks to load the beets onto horse-drawn wagons. The beets were deep in the earth and it took tremendous effort to pry them loose. We were weak from malnutrition, and by noon of the first day our hands were bleeding. My friend was in better shape than I was, and not nearly so done in. "You do what you like," I told him as we walked back to the farmhouse for lunch, "but I can't manage. Look at my hands."

"I'm still okay," he said, "but if you have to quit, I'm going too."

Just then the other owner came over to me. "From now on you'll be in charge of the cows. You'll be told what to do." I accepted this new assignment gladly, and slept contentedly in the barn with my cows for the next eight months.

I took care of the cows and the whole dairy as well. Usually, I had to get the hay ready and load it. I was badly exploited, working twelve hours a day for a few dollars a month and lousy food. The older brother was at least agreeable, but the younger one was plain mean, stupid and brutal. I used to fantasize about punching him in the nose, but I never did it. I had to earn enough money to get away and find something better.

I don't really regret those eight months. Working on the land is healthy and satisfying and I had never worked with my hands before. I got back some measure of physical strength and even acquired a bit of patience.

When I had saved about two hundred and fifty dollars I left. My companion had already quit. I went to the Employment Office in Laon and found a better-paying and safer job in Resigny as a wagon driver at one of the processing plants of a huge dairy company. Each morning I drove a wagon all around the neighborhood, collecting about two thousand gallons of milk. I got back to the plant about noon. The milk was processed, and in the afternoon it was loaded onto trucks in cans and early the next morning sold in Paris. It was pleasant work, especially in the summer. The Ardennes forest reminded me a little of my native Caucasus. I planned to stay long enough to save five hundred dollars and then try my luck in Paris.

I used to subscribe to a Paris newspaper to keep up with what was going on in the rest of the world. And since I was absorbed by the affairs of the Russian émigrés, I also took the two most important Russian-language papers that were published in Paris. But all this time I was thinking more and more seriously about "my" treasure . . . the treasure of the White Army.

It was crucial for me to understand the interconnections between the various groups of émigrés to figure out whom I could eventually go to for help to recover at least part of the treasure. I had already made one firm decision: I would not offer the treasure, or any part of it, to the exiled Russian military organizations. These organizations had sprung up everywhere, under the leadership of General Wrangel. Later, after his death in 1928, General Koutiepov assumed the role of leader. But the Civil War was over. We were defeated and in exile. All we could do now was to adjust to our new circumstances and understand that there was no possibility of overthrowing the Soviet regime from abroad. General Koutiepov and all the exiled class of officers dreamed of nothing else; I shared their passions, needless to say, but I had come to terms with reality. Many Russians, blinded by their hatred of Bolshevism, could not understand that aggressive action against the communist government from abroad would only reinforce the regime. The White organizations were riddled with provocateurs and double agents; even General Skoblin, who had commanded one of the most brilliant of the White regiments, had betrayed us. General Koutiepov and his successor, General Miller, were both kidnapped, to the consternation of the French press. What kind of organizations were these, whose leaders could be kidnapped in broad daylight in the middle of Paris? I was not going to share a single kopek with any of them. I would go after a part of the treasure and try to recover enough to finance a full-scale expedition. Then I would share it with the Russian schools, our disabled veterans and the Russian churches.

In the meantime, there I was at Resigny and the drudgery at the dairy plant. The manager was a bastard. He paid us eighty dollars a month, though we got enough to eat and a decent place to sleep. But I noticed that he preferred non-French-speaking employees and I soon discovered why. He was cheating us. Each month as we received our pay, we signed for it on a list. I noticed that he kept his finger over the place next to each name. Finally, one day, I had had enough, and I pushed his hand out of my way. He was cheating each of us out of one hundred francs. Eleven of us at one hundred francs apiece each month . . . not bad! I went to the manager and told him, "Monsieur, either you pay us what you owe us, or I'm going to write to your superiors in Paris."

The next day, he called me into his office. "Okay, I'll pay you but not the Polaks."

"No, either you pay everybody or I'm going to report you."

I realized, of course, that after this I could not stay on under any circumstances. Finally, he gave me my missing back pay for seven months. The Polish workers were afraid of losing their jobs so they settled for the one hundred francs that had been "omitted" from their last wages. I said good-bye and went on my way.

I knew that a former Russian soldier was the manager of a plant about twelve miles from Laon that rented farm equipment out to the local farmers. I got a job as a tractor driver and worked at harvesting the wheat near Vervins. It was summer and the life was so pleasant that I didn't give a thought to the treasure. When the harvesting was finished, I worked at plowing with the same machine.

By now I had saved what I had planned on, but I decided to accumulate a bit more. I didn't know Paris, and I was both attracted and intimidated. How would I manage in that vast city with no friends or acquaintances? So when the plowing was finished, I took a job in a nearby sugar-processing plant. Toward the end of November, as I was going about my work one day, I saw two foremen and two policemen approaching.

"Are you Sergei Orel? Do you have an identity card?"

I gave him my card. "Okay, get your belongings and come along."

"But why?"

"We have a warrant from Laon for your arrest. You are accused of stealing." I was terrified.

"But there must be some mistake. I've stolen nothing."

"You can tell that to the judge. We are only carrying out our instructions."

The gendarmes were riding bicycles, so I had to trot along between them. They didn't handcuff me; they were quite decent to me, in fact.

It was a Saturday, so I had to spend two days in the police station before I could be transferred to the Laon jail. The jail was in an ancient monastery, with thick walls and long corridors. I was outraged at being held as a suspect without trial, much less a sentence. According to the law, work in prison is optional, but I was put to work as soon as I arrived. The building was freezing cold — it hadn't been heated in centuries — and was almost unbearable once the sun had gone down. We were made to get into our nightclothes and march double time over the cold stone floors to our dormitory. Once we were inside, the doors were locked and nothing could move the guards to open them. After several days, I was at last called before the judge for a preliminary hearing. Before he said a word, I demanded to know why I was being held.

He replied, "I have issued a warrant against you on a complaint that you robbed a worker at the Maggi Dairy at Resigny."

The theft had supposedly occurred on a Sunday, over a month before; a suitcase belonging to one of the workers had disappeared. I asked how I came to be accused and the judge informed me that the manager had suggested that I was the guilty party.

I explained to the judge why the manager might wish to get even with me, and that at the time of the theft I had been forty miles away from the scene. To be absolutely sure of my alibi, I asked for a day so that I could figure out *exactly* where I had been that Sunday. I sat up all night doping it out, and by morning I had it all fitted together. At the time of the alleged crime, I had been playing billiards with Cassart, a former military policeman. I reported back to the judge and he promised to call Cassart. Cassart backed me up, and twenty days after I had been arrested, the judge let me go.

I was released just before Christmas. After that experience, with more than twenty-five hundred francs in my pocket, life looked rosy. I took the train for Paris and settled into a hotel near the Gare du Nord. I was fascinated by Paris. For the first three days I hardly slept. I wanted to see everything.

Then it was time to think about finding work and lodgings. I had the address of a Russian who had worked at the Resigny dairy and was now working at Joinville-le-Pont and lived on the Quai de la Marne. I moved into a small hotel near him. I still had twenty-two hundred francs left after my Parisian "extravagances." Instead of looking for a job right away, I decided to get a driver's license. That way I would have a skill to sell instead of having to apply as an unskilled worker.

In a month I had obtained my license both for pleasure driving and for trucks and I found a job as a truck driver at a mill near Troyes. The pay was good, although the work was hard. I had to load and unload hundred-pound sacks of flour. I intended to keep the job for only a few months, as all I needed was enough money to work out a scheme to get at the treasure. I would spend everything I had, my money and my strength, to get my hands on that treasure. I had had enough deprivation.

When I got back to Paris, I had almost five thousand francs, a good suit and overcoat. I was quite presentable. Again I settled in Joinville-le-Pont, which was then a charming little town. Since automobiles were rare in those days, most Parisians spent Sundays and holidays in the towns around Paris, especially Nogent-sur-Marne and Joinville, where there were plenty of nice restaurants and taverns. I moved into a little hotel and the man who owned it became a good friend. He only charged me sixteen francs a day for a very nice room and full board, including wine.

I began to look up people I had known in Russia who were now living in Paris, preferably civilians or acquaintances of my family. That took some time, as there were an enormous number of Russians spread all over Paris. I finally met the former district attorney of St. Petersburg, who had known both my father and grandfather. He was almost fifty years older than I but he seemed to enjoy my company. We met regularly to have dinner and to gossip.

I began to realize that my friend knew many important Parisians. I decided to tell him about the treasure after swearing him to reveal not a word about it to anyone, even if he decided not to help me.

"I believe I can help you, though," he told me. "But, before introducing you to the person I have in mind, I want you to understand that he is a very important man and won't get mixed up in anything that could hurt his reputation. But I have known him for a long time and he is very pro-Russian, and I think he will help."

After I had given it some thought, I told him: "I don't think it is necessary to tell him where the treasure came from. It would be wiser to tell him that it had belonged to my family."

I saw him a few days later. "Everything is okay," he told me. "The person I was telling you about is the Marquis de Navailles, chief of the European department of the French Foreign Ministry. He will receive you in a few days. If he agrees to help, under no circumstances offer him any reward. He would kick you out."

A few days later I was ushered into the office of M. de Navailles. He was a big man, with a ruddy complexion and exquisite manners, an eighteenth-century aristocrat. I told him my tale. He agreed to help me "on condition that your story is true." I assured him that no embarrassment would come to him. He gave me a personal letter to the French ambassador at Sofia, asking him to accept a package from me and to forward it to him. He also gave me a letter to the police requesting a French passport for me. That very day I received my passport and a visa for Bulgaria. The only problem that remained was money, and somehow the former prosecutor found another five thousand francs for me. I was on my way to the treasure.

11

The Treasure Stays Where It Was

I TOOK THE ORIENT EXPRESS for Bulgaria in January 1927. The winter had been severe in France, and I was hoping it would be warmer in southern Europe. But it was even colder there.

Hoping the weather would warm up, I delayed a few days in Sofia. But it did not change and I had to keep moving to avoid arousing the suspicions of the Bulgarian police, who took careful note of the arrival of every foreigner. I couldn't stay in my hotel just doing nothing. So I told the desk clerk, who was undoubtedly a police agent, that I had to go to Plovdiv, the second most important city in the country, to look into the tobacco market there. Plovdiv is on the railroad line to Burgas. I spent a day purchasing my digging tools and work clothes and then continued on to Burgas. I could definitely not spend more than twenty-four hours in Burgas without arousing suspicion. Why would a foreigner come to such a small city, where there was nothing to do, in the dead of winter?

I arrived in Burgas in the morning and spent almost the whole day looking for a place to change my clothes. That night I went to the public park near the beach, which was deserted at that hour. In an icy wind, I changed into my work clothes, hopping up and down to keep from freezing. I checked my street clothes at the railroad station, drank some hot coffee, then set off to the first hiding place. It was growing colder and colder. In spite of my warm clothing, I was trembling like a leaf. A strong wind bit my face and slowed me down. I didn't reach even the nearest cache until nearly midnight, and then it took me a half hour to locate it with a flashlight. Everything was in order; no one had discovered our secret. I tested the ground. It was frozen hard as a rock. I tried to dig, not at the actual site, so as not to betray it, but a little distance away. Useless. It would take dynamite to break the ground. I was furious that all my effort, my long trip, had been in vain. I would return to Paris empty-handed.

In the morning, half-frozen, I returned to Burgas and took the train to Sofia. Before returning to my hotel, I went to the public baths to change my clothes. The frigid weather continued; there was no way of knowing when it would end and I couldn't stay where I was. I returned to Paris.

My friend, the former prosecutor, was disappointed with me. I gave him my passport and M. de Navailles' letter and asked him to explain to Navailles why I had failed. I was worried about the money he had loaned me. I did not know whether he had borrowed it from someone else. One night, as I tossed and turned in bed trying to find a solution, I decided to go see my former commander, General Postovsky, who was a great gambler. The next day I went around and asked him to take me to his gambling club that evening. I needed to make some profit on my last thousand francs.

"You've come at a bad time," he said. "I've had a losing streak for a week and I've lost more than fifty thousand francs. All I have left is three thousand. But if you wish, come along. I'll try, but I make no promises."

I gave him my wallet and he played baccarat for both of us. By 2 A.M. he had won seventy thousand francs for himself and more than twenty thousand for me. I practically had to drag him away from the table.

I returned the money I had borrowed and went to Joinville to rest. I regretted that I had been so precipitate. I should have waited for spring to go to Bulgaria. The next expedition time I would plan more carefully. And I would need a companion.

After a few days of relaxation, I decided to get started doing something. I knew that Lieutenant General Rafalovitch, who was a former commander of the Cossack cavalry and a good friend of my family, was living in Brussels, He was a man of absolute integrity and loyalty. I went to see him. He was very glad to see me but I did not tell him about the treasure right away. I waited for about a month and then I told him the whole story. He listened to me carefully.

"I have been expecting you to speak to me about this business. I've heard some rumors about a war treasure taken out of Russia by General Pokrovsky. They say that you know where it is. Some people even claim that it has been in your possession since Pokrovsky's death. I am glad that you have told me the true story. You must realize that you are in a very delicate and dangerous position. If either the Reds or Whites ever become convinced that you know where the treasure is, your life will be in danger. They will kidnap you, torture you to obtain the secret, and then they will kill you."

"I've thought of all that," I replied. "But that still wouldn't give them any chance at all of finding the treasure. Even if I gave someone a detailed description of the general location, they still couldn't find the exact spot without digging up the entire area, about twelve square miles. Once I was dead, no one could find it."

"All right," he said, "I'm convinced. But what are you going to do?" I explained in detail my plan to recover the treasure and what I intended to do with it afterward. He asked for a few days to think it over.

When I returned, he said, "I have concluded that you are right. I agree that it would not be wise to talk to the Russian authorities in Paris. In the first place, they couldn't do anything without your help. And once they got their hands on it, it would disappear. Like you, I am against any attempt to attack the Bolsheviks from abroad. Furthermore, I believe you have demonstrated a right to the treasure. Keep me advised. I will try to help. But you must be careful; you will be in bad trouble if word gets around."

It was the spring of 1927 and it was to be two years

before I found just the right man. During those two years in Brussels I became administrative director of the famous Russian chorus, the Cossacks of Kuban. One day in Brussels I saw a man on the street dressed in the costume of the Kuban Cossacks. I could not believe my eyes — for as he came closer, I recognized George Vinnikov, a great old pal who had been in my regiment. We went into a café and he told me his story. Because he had had musical training, in Yugoslavia the *ataman* of the Kuban Cossacks, General Naoumenko, had commissioned him to form a Cossack choir. For several years the choir had remained in Yugoslavia but eventually it began to receive invitations to perform abroad. They were in Brussels to give three concerts. Naturally, I attended the opening night. The next day at lunch, Vinnikov remarked: "It would be so much more convenient if we had someone who knew this part of Europe and could speak the languages. I know only a bit of French and the rest speak nothing but Russian. We always have to find a translator." Then out of the blue, he said: "We need someone exactly like you. How about being our director?" I was taken by surprise and told him that I didn't know anything about that sort of business. "And," I said, "right now I don't have the kind of money to do a lot of traveling, and that would be necessary, wouldn't it?"

"Yes," he replied, "you would have to be our advance man, make all the arrangements, sign contracts, and so forth. But, naturally, you would be paid the same salary as I, and your expenses would be taken care of." I explained my difficulties with the police. "Listen, Nicholas," he replied, "I have known you for a long time and I know that you are incapable of dishonesty. We would be honored to have you." I agreed on condition that General Naoumenko give his approval, and I wrote him explaining my situation. Two weeks later I received a letter from the general confirming my appointment. I contacted all the great impresarios of Europe and arranged many appearances. The choir was a great success everywhere.

In 1929, a construction engineer of Russian descent, a man named Arian, introduced me to a Belgian diplomat, Baron K., a counselor at the Belgian embassy in a neighboring country. He had been stationed in St. Petersburg as a young man and had married a Russian woman. He agreed to help me get the treasure out of Bulgaria.

Arian knew only the bare outlines of the plan and I assured his silence by promising him a generous commission. Unfortunately, I did not realize that his business was in trouble and that he was deeply in debt. Our plan was for the baron to go to Bulgaria after me, receive a suitcase from me containing part of the treasure, and take it out of the country in the diplomatic pouch. In a few days he had obtained a passport and a Bulgarian visa for me under the name of Nansen. I was to leave first. We would register at different hotels in Sofia. I would proceed to Burgas, return to Sofia, meet the baron at the Belgian legation, and give him my suitcase.

I arrived in Sofia and waited four days, but there was no sign of the baron. I was frantic. At the legation I finally found a message. He had fallen ill en route and was in Belgrade. He asked me to wait in Sofia, as he hoped the doctor would allow him to move in two or three days. Four days later, another message arrived: he was worse and had to return to Brussels. He promised to continue our business when he had recovered.

This was a terrible blow. I went back immediately and visited the baron's bedside. He was very upset that he had been unable to complete his voyage. He promised again that we would resume our mission as soon as possible. I went to see Arian, who was very cool to me. I could not understand until he finally blurted out: "You know I don't believe a word of this story of the baron's sickness. I think this was a diplomatic illness. I think you carried off the affair and are keeping it from me so that you won't have to pay me my share."

"You are out of your mind," I told him. "Even if you don't believe me, do you really think the baron would risk his reputation and career for a few pennies? Go ask him yourself."

I learned later that he had indeed gone to the baron, who had thrown him out of the house.

A week later I was arrested on a charge of suspicion of swindling. Arian had brought an accusation against me to the Belgian police. The story was all over the papers.

I protested, of course, but I was held for thirty days. Six months later, the case was dismissed for lack of evidence, but my reputation was ruined. No end of false stories had appeared in the Belgian press and the police had sent inquiries about me to a number of other countries. There was nothing on the books against me anywhere, but I was labeled undesirable and effectively barred from several countries forever. This was a ghastly situation for a stateless person.

I had not a cent, no means of leaving the country much

less reaching Bulgaria. I was near the end of my rope
when I found a jeweler who was willing to lend me the
twenty thousand francs I needed for my next expedition. I
put it in a bank while I made my preparations and waited
for my chance to go back to Bulgaria.

Then one morning I received a summons to appear before the police. I was accused once again of swindling.
The jeweler had decided that I might be going to skip out
with his money, and instead of asking for it back, he had
gone straight to the police. When I heard what the accusation was, I immediately wrote him out a check, but I was
condemned to a month in prison anyhow. I appealed the
sentence, but the appeals court sustained the sentence *in
absentia* since I was out of the country at the time. When
I returned, I found that I was to be deported. I had either
to leave immediately or face an indeterminate sentence.

I was desperate to get hold of some money and a passport that would get me into Bulgaria. I wrote a friend of
mine, a former Russian officer who was living in Switzerland, and asked him if there was any way I could borrow
fifty thousand Belgian francs. I promised to pay him back
double that amount. He was an old friend and I knew he
would trust me. He wrote back that he didn't have such a
sum but knew someone who would lend it to me if he
guaranteed the loan. He would arrange for me to meet
this person in France.

I entered France via Luxembourg and had a meeting
with this man. A few days later the money came; I was
obliged to return it in three months. Now I had to obtain
a real passport, not a forged one. I had heard that this

could be arranged at some of the consulates in Berlin. I went there with a Belgian woman friend. She suggested that she go around to the consulates. They might be nicer to her than to me.

I waited for her all one day while she inquired around. Finally, she returned. "Done," she said. "You have your passport." She had been to a half-dozen consulates. When she had told them that she wanted a passport for a friend, some of the officials had simply laughed at her, others were angered. She was ready to come back empty-handed when she had passed a sign that said "Consulate of Panama." She had decided to give it one more try. The consul had received her courteously and listened to her. He finally told her to have me come in person. I was leery of a trap but there was nothing else I could think of to do.

He was very hospitable. As character witnesses, I was able to give him the names of two persons living in Berlin whom he knew. A few days later I received my passport, for which I paid thirty thousand Belgian francs.

There was no question of entering Bulgaria officially, since the passport carried my real name. I went to the Yugoslav border town of Zajecar, hoping to find someone to get me across the border. I finally found two men who agreed for three thousand dinars. Meanwhile, I stayed with my uncle, who was a supervisor at the copper mines about eighteen miles away. One day the men who were to smuggle me across saw my wallet bulging with money. They exchanged glances, and I decided I had to be more cautious.

At last, we set out one midnight, walking for a couple of

hours. Finally, my guides told me we were three miles inside Bulgaria and it was time for me to pay up. I handed over the money, and while they were counting it, put my hand on the pistol in my coat pocket. As I had half expected, they both pulled knives and demanded my money, watch and ring. I made a motion as if I were reaching for my wallet, but instead pulled my gun and put a bullet in each of their heads, then I ran like hell. About a half mile farther on I threw my pistol into a stream. As I was walking along the road to Vidin, following the course of the Danube, I ran into a patrol of five policemen who demanded to know why I had fired my gun. I answered that I did not even have a gun. They searched me but decided to take me to Vidin for questioning anyhow. This arrest put an end to my elaborate plans.

Of course, I denied that I had anything to do with killing the two men, whose bodies had since been discovered, and the police admitted freely that they were not really concerned about that. They were just as happy to have two fewer smugglers to worry about. After two days, I was transferred to the prison in Sofia. The police there were most anxious to know whether I had entered Bulgaria illegally. I made up an elaborate story which they did not believe. The fact was I had mailed my Panamanian passport to General Delivery in Burgas and by this time it had already been returned to Brussels.

It was a disaster. The man who had loaned me his money, not having heard from me for so long, had naturally concluded that I had run off with it and he denounced me to the police. A short time later he died.

When I finally got back to Switzerland by way of Yugo-slavia, I was arrested and extradited to France. Later, I was cleared of the charge he had made.

I was getting desperate. I would do anything to reach the treasure. I decided that the first thing I needed was a good lawyer. Through an acquaintance I was recommended to one in The Hague. I sold a camera and my gold watch to get the money to visit him. I will call him simply Leon. We struck up a friendship right off the bat. After I had told him the whole story, including my problems with the law, he said he would help me. He was quite rich and did not need any money. I believe the romantic, adventurous side of the undertaking appealed to him. He agreed to finance my first expedition; after that, I would have enough money to pay for a hundred.

12

Leon

IT WAS THE MIDDLE OF SUMMER and we decided to get started right away. We had a simple and workable plan. We would go by train to Constanza in Rumania and sail from there to Constantinople. I had not been in Turkey for a long time and, we hoped, would not be recognized. I was to stay in Constantinople for a few days, and then take the boat alone to Burgas, do my job, and telegraph Leon in Constantinople. He would get on the Orient Express, which goes through Bulgaria on its way to Paris, having wired me in care of General Delivery at Plovdiv. I would be waiting at that station and would pass the package to him. In those days the Orient Express was all first class and the border guards treated the passengers with deference; his bags would not be opened until he reached Paris, and he would get off before that. I would take a boat up the Danube and meet him in Lausanne.

The day of my departure arrived. The boat, the *Bulgaria*, was in the middle of the Bosporus, and I was the only passenger. I was rowed out by some Turkish sailors. The sea was so rough that I almost lost my passport as I climbed the ladder to get on board. Since I was supposed to be a Panamanian, I could not speak Russian or show that I understood Bulgarian. I managed to communicate with the crew in German and English.

When I arrived in Burgas, I checked into a hotel and let it be known that I was waiting three days for the departure of my boat from Routschouk. I spent my first day there on the beach and that night went fishing. (This would explain my overnight absence from the hotel the following night.) I decided to go after the treasure on the second day.

That night was warm and there was a full moon. I got to the hiding place nearest the city about 1 A.M. After digging for about an hour and a half, I found the cases. We had marked them to indicate the contents. The first contained jewels. The next contained securities and English currency.

I took the jewels and papers and replaced the cases, and covered over the trenches so that no one could tell that there had been any digging. I returned to Burgas without incident and buried my tools on the beach. I knew it would be difficult to get back into the hotel without arousing suspicion about my package, since I had departed empty-handed to "go fishing." So I left the package at the door, and as I entered I asked the desk clerk to fetch me a bottle of wine. Then I ran back for the package, carried it to my room, and hid it under the bed.

Next I wired Leon as agreed, and by evening I had his

answer. He would pass through Plovdiv in two days. Now was my first opportunity to examine what I had. There were beautiful jewels, about one hundred grams of cut but unset diamonds, about one hundred foreign bonds, and twenty-five thousand pounds sterling in currency.

The next day I took the train to Plovdiv. I went to the station the next day and saw Leon debark from the train. This was the moment of danger: I had to pass the bags to him inconspicuously. He took them and said, "Everything is all right. I sent the steward for a bottle of mineral water." This was our entire conversation. It was ten days before I saw him again, in Lausanne. When he arrived there he had deposited the treasure in a bank. The operation had been a marvelous success — but it was not over yet. We had to exchange the money and sell the bonds and the jewels. Leon was a tremendous help because he had so many contacts. All this took two months, but brought us a handsome sum.

When the expedition had finally worked out so well, I went back to Brussels illegally and renewed contact with some old and faithful friends. Naturally I shared some of my wealth with the Cossacks of Kuban. But nothing lasts forever. Several years later my friend Lieutenant Vinnikov, founder and guiding spirit of the choir, fell ill and died in Brussels, and without him the choir split up into several groups. A quintet managed by the talented Svetlanov brothers from the chorus enjoyed some success in Europe for a number of years, but that was the end of the Cossacks of Kuban.

After our successful expedition in Bulgaria Leon and I traveled a good deal, particularly to Vienna, our favorite city, but also to Berlin, Prague and Budapest. While we were enjoying ourselves, however, we never lost sight of the fact that we were going to recover the rest of the treasure. We had long since decided that the only effective way to get at it was to go to Bulgaria as tourists on a yacht and that we would have to buy one, rather than rent it, so that we wouldn't be saddled with a crew we couldn't trust.

We searched for the right vessel for over a month and grew discouraged. One was too large, another too small. One day Leon received a letter from a friend in Rotterdam telling him that the kind of boat he was looking for was anchored at Cannes. We went there immediately and fell in love with the yacht at first sight. Leon went to England and bought it, retaining its registration, which was Panamanian. Many yachts had this registration, but it was a lucky detail because of my passport. It was perfect for us. It had two powerful engines, six cabins and quarters for a crew of five.

It took us two months to get ready. The most complicated task was to find a reliable crew. We put together an international team: three Dutch sailors, a German mechanic and his wife, who would serve as maid, a Russian cook and an English captain. Leon deliberately chose a crew who did not understand French so that we could talk freely. We took on board a great supply of all sorts of provisions and invited two beautiful women we knew to add the proper touch of posing as rich tourists on a cruise.

We departed in midsummer, sailing at a leisurely pace.
We stayed at Naples for three days and visited the famous
Blue Grotto on the isle of Capri to please our companions,
and a few days later we stopped for a few hours at Lemnos, where I had had so many adventures, to buy some
fruit and fresh bread. After a two-day stopover at Constantinople we headed toward the Bulgarian coast. First,
we anchored at Varna, a larger and more pleasant city
than Burgas, as it might have looked suspicious if we had
gone directly to Burgas, bypassing a tourist attraction like
Varna. We spent a week there, lolling on the beach.

Finally, we headed for Burgas. The customs officials did
not bother us; they were concerned only with those who
actually arrived in port. We moved back and forth from
the boat with sacks and bags to get them used to our
moving about. I found my tools where I had buried them
on the first expedition. To explain our overnight absence
to the ladies and the captain, we said that we were going
to visit Russian friends of mine who lived inland.

We set out early the first evening. I carried my Mauser,
though Leon was unarmed. Even though the first hiding
place was still half full, I decided to go straight to the
second, and we got there about 11 P.M. An hour later, we
had finished. But I was only able to take out about half
the valuables because Leon was scared and kept urging
me to hurry. I realized that for the next expedition I
would need a different kind of man; you can't ask a bour-
geois lawyer to be an adventurer, specially when the
affair had little or no heroism to it. We were back at the
seashore at about 2 A.M. and had located the place where

I was planning to hide the tools. We buried the tools and rested a while. Then we started out at a leisurely pace. We didn't want to get to town too early.

After walking for about ten minutes, we heard *"stoi"* ("halt"). That's it, I said to myself, the customs police. I had forgotten that the customs would patrol that part of the beach at night since it was an ideal spot for smugglers to land. The voice came from the brush at the edge of the beach. I sized up the situation immediately: if we remained on the beach we were done for. I told Leon to follow me and ran for the cover of the brush. We heard the order to halt again but by this time we were hidden. We were each carrying a bag full of valuables. "Run toward the town and wait for me near the station," I said to Leon. I decided to fire on the police if they pursued us. A few seconds later, the customs man (who, as I had surmised, was alone) fired in the air; I fired two shots in his direction and he apparently decided to leave us alone.

I reached Burgas without any trouble and found Leon at a bistro near the station. He was gray. "I'm not a Cossack, you know," he told me. We bought a few pieces of fruit and some vegetables and put them into our sacks. When we passed the customs officials at the port, they greeted us as casually as usual, and we reached the boat without any difficulty. I put the sacks into a storage space near my cabin that I always kept closed. No one noticed them.

We spent the next day on the beach and the following day we left Burgas for Constantinople. We decided that we had to be alone to take inventory of what we had, so we put the women off the boat in Trieste, in spite of their tears and protests, and gave them money to go back to Brussels. We cruised around the boot of Italy and left the boat at San Remo, then made our way to Switzerland by train. Once again, thanks to his connections, Leon was able to sell everything. After our business was done, Leon had to return to The Hague to take care of some business.

Even after I had given away about three-quarters of the money from my last expedition, I still had quite a bit. However, I knew that war was imminent and I was determined to get back to Bulgaria as soon as possible. Leon tried to dissuade me, listing all the difficulties that the tense political situation would create. I knew he was right, but I couldn't accept a quiet life. He offered to lend me whatever I needed to get established in Brussels, but I could not undertake any legitimate business, since I had no legal documents with my real name. I decided to go to Bulgaria one more time. Alone.

13

From Riches to Ruin

AT THE END OF FEBRUARY of 1939 I set out by train for Naples, and went from there to Constantinople by ship. Then I had to figure out some way of getting into Bulgaria. I met an old acquaintance there by chance, the ex–police chief of my hometown. He imported hams from Bulgaria and he went back and forth to Burgas all the time. The hams were shipped on Turkish feluccas, which sailed to Sozopol, a city south of Burgas, to collect wood. Of course, he knew the captains of all these boats, so I had him introduce me to a couple and I made arrangements to go to Burgas on one boat and come back on another.

The morning I arrived in Burgas I found the fourth hiding place, the closest one to where we had landed. Everything came off without a hitch. As before, I took only part of what was buried. This time I managed three of the six cases, as well as three unopened cases in each of the other three hiding places — twelve cases in all, still a sizable fortune. The felucca I was to return on was not ready to leave, so for the next five days I helped load it. We got back to Constantinople without incident and I managed to slip by customs. I still had my room in the Pera Palace Hotel.

I had so many valuables with me that I thought it would be prudent to deposit some of them, mainly the stocks and some of the diamonds, in a bank vault and plan to come back for them later, and so I did this. I was worried that I would be thoroughly searched at customs in Naples. That did not turn out to be the case, surprisingly, and I made my way peacefully to Leon's home in The Hague. He was grateful to see me safe and sound, and confessed that he had been very concerned. However, he refused to go back to Constantinople to recover what I had put in the bank, which put me in a very difficult position. Convinced that war was imminent, I wrote to the bank and asked them to advise me how I could authorize a person to open my safe deposit box. They wrote back with instructions on how to proceed. Leon still refused to go, so I had to go to Constantinople by myself. He advised me to find a buyer, at least for the diamonds; I could leave the stocks in the Constantinople branch office of any of the major European banks.

At Anvers I located a diamond merchant who agreed to make the trip, and who was ready to buy the diamonds from me on the spot. I drove across Germany, Austria, and Hungary and as far as Belgrade with my new Belgian girl friend. The merchant, who was Jewish, didn't want to travel through these countries, so he took the Orient Express and met us in Belgrade. We all spent a very pleasant evening the first night we were there and then agreed to meet early the next morning. My girl friend and I arrived on time for our appointment. But the diamond merchant was late, and when he arrived he acted very disturbed and announced that he had to return home immediately. I protested vigorously, but then, because I knew that his concern had to do with the persecution of the Jews by the Germans, I did not insist further.

I phoned Leon to tell him that I would have to return to The Hague because the merchant could not continue on with me. He told me instead to go to Budapest and that he would join me there. So my girl and I went there and settled into a hotel in the heart of the city, on the charming island in the Danube. The manager knew me, since I had stayed there several times before. One day, I saw him wearing an army officer's uniform and when I asked him about it, he explained that the political situation was very grave and that the government had mobilized some of the reservists. That evening he came to our room and advised me to leave the country immediately. "If war breaks out," he said, "you will be stuck here, and if America comes in, you are bound to be interned." We decided that this was good advice and that we should leave immediately. If war did break out and I was caught with a phony passport, I could be arrested as a spy. We left Budapest on August 25, 1939, one week before the war began. It took us a long time to reach the Luxembourg border. All the roads in Austria and Germany were clogged with military convoys. When we finally reached the Moselle and the bridge that connects Luxembourg and Germany, a nasty surprise was waiting for us. No one was being permitted across. We had to sit there all day before we were finally allowed to go over. The next day we reached Brussels. Immediately I went to the beautiful apartment I had there, furnished with rare Russian books, icons, and other objets d'art. An old girl friend was living there as housekeeper, since she was out of work. I decided I'd better stay off the streets, as there were all sorts of rumors about German parachutists and spies and I did not want to take the chance of being taken for one. Then I had a piece of bad luck (or was it good fortune in disguise?). The woman who had traveled with me to Budapest phoned to say that her stepfather, who was a French citizen, had just been mobilized and was to return right away to France. She very much wanted me to meet him before he left and, against my better judgment, I agreed. I walked the half mile that separated my apartment from hers and when I was almost there, three men approached and showed me their badges. One said: "Police. Let me have your papers, please."

When I reached into my pocket, my heart almost stopped. My passport was not there. I had not taken the time to transfer it from another coat. But I couldn't tell the police that, because I was renting the apartment under a different name from the one on the passport. The only thing I could think of to do was to say I had left it at my hotel. The police said I had better come along to the station house and explain everything to the officer in charge. They would send someone to my hotel to find the passport. But when I got to the magistrate, I decided I had better tell the truth, especially since he knew me. "This is going to cost you a month in jail," he said, "since you have already been formally expelled from the country once." So I found myself in jail again, cursing my carelessness.

The next day I appeared before the judge to be arraigned. Much to my surprise, he greeted me cheerfully. When I asked him why he was so cheerful, he replied that he had just signed a warrant for my arrest on a charge of swindling. "Do you know Mr. ————?" It was the diamond merchant. Now it dawned on me why he had left so precipitately in Belgrade. An associate of his had gone to the police looking for information about me. Needless to say, he had found out that I had been accused of swindling twice and had been expelled from Belgium. He had warned his friend to get away from me as soon as possible. Since the diamond merchant had not suffered any losses at my hands, he was willing to drop the whole matter. But the law followed its inexorable course. The judge had presented an indictment on the grounds that I had wished to swindle the man and I was sentenced to eighteen months in prison. I appealed, and that charge was finally dismissed; but I was still charged and convicted of using a false name when I had written to the merchant.

To add to my woes, I received another sentence of four months in prison for something I had not done. It had all begun a year before when I met a pretty girl one evening at the movies. I had walked her home and we had agreed to meet again. A few days later, we went to see another film that was restricted to adults. When she was asked for her identity card, she said she had forgotten it and so I guaranteed the ticket taker that she was nineteen, which is what she had told me. Later, as we were having a drink in a café, I caught a glimpse of her card when she opened her pocketbook. I was shocked to see that she was only sixteen, and decided not to see her again. (Belgian law is very strict on the corruption of minors.) I told her I was going off on a long trip. Then one day while I was serving my sentence in prison in Brussels, I was called to court and there she was. She had testified that I had seduced her. I learned only later that she had bragged to her friends about having had an affair with a rich foreigner and that one of her friends had told her parents, and that they had gone to the police. Having started the whole mess with lies, she couldn't stop lying now. I was found guilty.

As the war began to rage in earnest, food grew scarce and life in prison was a nightmare. We were given only a little bread with some margarine melted into it and warm water. I became so undernourished that my legs and feet swelled up horribly and I had to be transferred to the prison hospital. The food was better there and after a month I was all right. I was told by the police that I was to be detained even after my sentence ran out, because I was considered a menace to the public order.

Each day we strolled in the prison courtyard, I saw members of the Gestapo. They had taken over part of the jail for their own prisoners. I knew that if I told them my real name and that I had been an officer of the White Army, I could get free. And after a while a German officer did come to the library, where I was in charge, to inspect the books. I told him I was a Russian and how it was that I had ended up in prison. He found my story incredible. "You're out of your mind to stay here," he told me, and he offered to let me go right away if I would take a job with the German authorities; my knowledge of languages would make me very useful. It was July 1941, a few days after the German invasion of Russia. I refused. I knew what the Germans were doing to my country.

But just about this time, I had the luck to be transferred to a minimum-security prison that had been built for emotionally disturbed people along with all the other foreign prisoners.

I was treated quite differently from the other prisoners. The camp director had decided that my sentence was unjust, and although he did not have the authority to do anything about it, he made me librarian there and gave me complete freedom to come and go as I pleased. I could have escaped at any time and I often thought of doing so, but I decided against it because I did not want to betray the director's trust. One horrifying day the Germans discovered that there were some Jews among us; they quickly transferred them to German camps. My hatred for the Belgian authorities made me reluctant to do anything for that country, but I did help the Belgian resistance in one small way. Near the prison there were some mines where the Germans forced Russian prisoners of war to work. Many of them used to escape and join the partisans. I used to write notes in Russian which the Belgian underground would give them, urging them to tell the Germans nothing if they were captured.

Soon, I had terrible news. The woman whom I had left

in charge of my apartment had never communicated with me in any way, in spite of my many letters. Finally I appealed to the authorities to get in touch with her. The news came back that she had sold all my beautiful possessions and that I had nothing left.

But soon after that, at last something good happened. I received a postcard in Russian, mailed from Brussels, from a woman I didn't know. She had heard of my plight and wanted to help. Even before I had finished writing her a letter, I was summoned to the director's office. A magnificent package of bread, chocolate, tea, sugar, brandy and cigarettes had arrived from her. We corresponded all through my internment, and I learned that she was the wife of the proprietor of the most elegant Russian café in Brussels. I did not know what she looked like, whether she was old or young, pretty or not. I asked her for a picture and discovered that in fact she was young and lovely. She used to complain about her husband in her letters. So I decided to go on the offensive. I wrote her a love letter. For a week I was in agony, not knowing how she would respond. Then one day to my great surprise, I was summoned to the visiting room, and there she was. We fell into each other's arms and that began a love that was to last for eight years.

14

The Soviets and I

ON SEPTEMBER 14, 1944, after a short battle, the English occupied Rekam, near the prison. All night German and Allied shells crisscrossed overhead. The fighting was so close that we could hear a burst of artillery fire from one side and an explosion on the other almost simultaneously. We were near the Siegfried Line, which the Americans were bombing constantly. A few months later, on January 1, 1945, the Germans launched a last desperate air offensive. The furniture and buildings trembled and danced but we were not hit.

The clock had struck the hour of freedom but for me it was canceled out by an arbitrary and cruel decision. My conduct in camp had been exemplary; it was attested to by both the director and Father Stefan Gervais, a Franciscan friar to whom I had given Russian lessons. Nonetheless, the police gave me one month to leave the country under threat of being reinterned. I was refused the status of political refugee to which I had a legal right, and was a stateless person.

Back in Brussels I found my benefactress. She had taken a small apartment for the two of us. At last I felt sure I had someone by my side who loved me for myself, not because I was rich or handsome or exotic. After she had left her husband, she had bought a laundry and she had worked there day and night to keep us going. My beloved Maroussia told me also that somebody else, a man I did not know, had intervened with the Belgian authorities to get me released. Victor Breslav was a Russian engineer who had lived in Belgium since before World War I and was a top executive in a large plant. After the Liberation he had applied for Soviet citizenship, and was subsequently elected secretary-general of the Union of Soviet Patriots in Belgium. When he had heard about me through Father Gervais, he had informed the authorities that he would guarantee me a job at the union. Needless to say, I was hesitant to go to work for those who had for so long been my mortal enemies. But things change, and patriotism perhaps does not depend entirely on who happens to rule one's country. Anyhow, I was desperate.

Working for the Soviets brought down on me the hatred and contempt of my fellow White Russian émigrés, even though my work was humanitarian and not political. My first job was to fill out forms for the Soviet Red Cross, which was trying to locate persons who had been forcibly transported by the Nazis and who might now be in territory occupied by the Russians. Most of the inquiries were for Jews. Sadly, I never found any of them, although we did locate some other Belgians. Later, I was put in charge of a small Russian language revue. As a result, I was identified in the Belgian, French and English press as a Soviet spy. I found this so ridiculous that I did not even try to refute the charge. How could anyone think the Soviets would use me as a spy — a former White officer, now so conspicuously in their employ?

A year went by after my liberation from prison camp and my life was poisoned by the police. Each month I had to go through the ordeal of having my Belgian visa extended for another month. Sometimes, it took days or even weeks. If my papers were to lapse before I got a renewal, I was in constant danger of being picked up as an illegal alien. Often I had to stay away from my own apartment for fear of being arrested. One day, when Maroussia and I were alone in the apartment, two plainclothes police came looking for me, and I had to hide behind a cabinet in the kitchen. They came so close I thought they might hear my breathing. Finally, after long efforts by some well-placed persons who had taken an interest in my case, I was granted the right to remain in Belgium. The Soviet commercial mission put Breslav and me in charge of an export-import operation for agricultural machines and produce. My material situation was immeasurably improved and we were able to move to a larger apartment and even buy a car.

I had no time to think about my treasure, and I had really given up all hopes of recovering it. Bulgaria was now communist and it would be all the more dangerous for me to take risks there. And now that I had found contentment with Maroussia, I had no desire to take up my former life of adventure.

Nevertheless, my love for my poor and hard-put country got me involved once again. In spite of the terrible sacrifices the Russian people had endured during the war, the USSR was the target of hate-filled propaganda. Some people were seriously proposing that Bolshevism could be exterminated because of Russia's weakness. I cared only for my people, who could not endure another bloodletting. I was obsessed by the thought that I could do something to help, and finally I believed I had found a way. Since it was chiefly Americans who were preaching a crusade against Russia, it was they whom I had to influence.

I composed a stenographic record of an imaginary top-secret meeting in the Kremlin attended by all the Russian military leaders and presided over by Stalin. I managed to give it a certain authenticity because I had had military training and because I had read every Soviet publication that came into Belgium. The supposed occasion for the meeting was a threat to the Soviet Union by its former allies, England and the United States. Stalin had called his military advisers together to determine the capabilities and preparedness of all units of the Soviet armed forces. The military men had made their reports with absolute frankness, and they all exhibited the greatest optimism. One of them had declared that the Soviet Union would have its own atomic bomb within a year. (I was absolutely astonished when this turned out to be true.) I thought the report sounded realistic and detailed, and that any potential enemy, having seen it, would think twice before attacking Russia. Now, I had to get it to the Americans.

My first thought was simply give it to them without asking for any money, but I concluded that I would not be credible. They had to believe that I was acting for a member of the Soviet consulate or embassy. So I approached an inspector of the Belgian security police whom I had previously met and told him that a Soviet diplomat who wished to defect had asked me to be his intermediary. I explained that he had authorized me to make the offer for him, because he knew there were Soviet agents in the American service and he wanted to remain in Europe. I asked for a million Belgian francs, half on delivery of the document and half a month later. This appeared to convince the inspector, who returned a few days later with an affirmative response from the Americans. He furnished me with a Russian alphabet typewriter, and while Maroussia worked each day in the Office of Repatriation, I typed out the "minutes." Finally I told the inspector to inform the Americans that the document was ready for delivery. The next day he informed me that someone would wait for me in a room in the Hotel des Boulevards and give me the first five hundred thousand francs. I was then to go to the Soviet consulate, pass the money on to the diplomat, and return to the hotel with the document.

As I entered the hotel room, I could see a large bundle under the bedspread. I had no way of carrying it except in my pockets, and I didn't know how I was going to manage that since I already had the document in my pocket and I was not going anywhere to pass the money on to anyone.

If I came back from the consulate with the money still on me, I would be found out. And I would surely be followed when I left the hotel. I did the only thing I could think of. I stuffed the money into my pockets and, just as I got to the door, I pulled the document out, handed it to the startled agent, and said, "I am going to pass the money on." He started to say something, but I was already half-way down the stairs.

Outside the hotel, I took a taxi to the consulate, followed by two cars.

When I arrived, I had the bad luck to run into the consul, Skobelov. "There you are," he said. "I want to talk to you for a few minutes. Take off your coat and come into my office." I couldn't refuse but I couldn't go in there with my pockets bulging with all those bills. "Excuse me a moment," I replied, "I have to have a few words with the secretary first. I'll be with you in a couple of minutes."

As Skobelov started upstairs to his office, I went out the front door onto the street. Pretending not to see the two cars that followed me, I crossed the avenue and took a streetcar that stopped a few steps from my home. I wrapped the money in oilcloth and buried it in the coal bin in the cellar.

Then I took the tram back to the hotel. The American agent was furious, and demanded to know why I had rushed out of the hotel. I said the reason was obvious. Clearly, he was not alone in the hotel and I was well aware that they could easily have taken the money back once they had the paper. He wanted to know why I had gone home after I left the consulate and I don't remember exactly how I got around that. It was clear that he did not believe me, but I felt it didn't make much difference. The only thing that mattered was that they couldn't prove the document was counterfeit.

Though they had promised not to try to find out the name of the Soviet diplomat who had sold the information, I was soon summoned by the Belgian inspector, who had been the original intermediary, to meet some American agents at the Hotel Metropole. They bombarded me with questions. I just kept saying that I knew nothing more than I had already told them, and I kept repeating that they had promised not to ask for the defector's name.

As we were talking, I heard a funny noise in the next room. I jumped up and threw all my weight against the door that opened into the adjoining room. This sent three inspectors of the Belgian security police, who had been listening at the door, sprawling to the floor and made the American agents furious. One called in two more colleagues. By this time, I had had quite enough. I had my pistol in my pocket and was ready to use it if I had to. I told them the affair was over and I did not wish to see any of them again. Thank God, they let me go. If they had tried to stop me, I would have shot them dead before they could have made a move and then I would have had to take refuge with the Soviets and been sent back to Russia.

I did not know then that the Soviets knew all about my history in the affair of the treasure.

Now I had quite a bit of money, though the Americans, as I expected, never paid me the second half. For some time my life went along without incident. I put the money in a bank vault so as not to arouse the suspicions of the Belgian police. After a few months I thought my income plus Maroussia's salary would be enough to explain an improved standard of living, so I bought a new car.

This peaceful situation was not to last, however. One evening we were at a meeting at the Union of Soviet Patriots hall in Brussels. As it was breaking up, Consul Skobelov rose to speak. "Comrades, I have some good news. The Presidium of the Supreme Soviet of the Soviet Union has authorized the return of one of our members — Nicholas Svidine." I thought I must be dreaming. Maroussia almost fainted. This was very mysterious and frightening. I was not even a Soviet citizen and it was common knowledge that I had been an officer in Wrangel's army. I certainly had not requested a passport. The audience applauded and everyone shook my hand. I accepted their congratulations and said nothing.

After the meeting, Maroussia and I went to see Breslav, who was the secretary-general of the union. He thought the whole thing was bizarre and agreed to go see the consul the next day. When he came back, the told me the consul demanded to see me personally. I asked him to accompany me.

When I arrived, the consul delivered the following speech: "We know with absolute certainty that you were in Bulgaria with General Pokrovsky at the time that he was killed by the Bulgarian police. We also know that he was in possession of a fortune which, of course, he had stolen from the Russian people. You are the only one who remains of his entourage and we also know that you have,

on occasion, sold large quantities of valuables and diamonds. We regard this as proof that you have knowledge
about the treasure, and what remains of it. Besides this,
we have the records of a counterrevolutionary group in
Germany that pursued you for two years, though they
failed to find you."

He was silent for a moment. I said nothing.

"Now you belong to the Union of Soviet Patriots. Since
you have lived abroad, you have committed no hostile act
against your country, and you have not been active in any
of the White organizations. During the war your behavior
was absolutely correct. We are aware that you were harassed by the Belgian police at the instigation of the
White Russian émigrés. Now, however, it is your duty to
give back to the Russian people what rightfully belongs to
them. It is for that reason that the Soviet Union invites
you to return. You will be paid back generously, and decorated. A few days from now a Soviet ship will stop at
Anvers and take you on board."

As I listened to all this, my first inclination was simply
to refuse. I hesitated. I thanked the consul for the goodwill of the Soviet government and asked for a few days to
think things over. Breslav, whose situation was delicate,
warned me to be very careful. Maroussia begged me to
refuse. This suggested a new tack.

The next day I went back to see the consul. I explained
that I was living with a Russian woman who was also a
member of the Union of Soviet Patriots. "You know, when
I think of how she saved my life during the war, I realize I
could never leave her here by herself."

The consul made it plain that this put him in a difficult position with his superiors. But after thinking it over for a few moments, he promised that she would be permitted to follow me shortly. "I will not go without her," I insisted.

For two months they left us alone. Finally, the consul summoned me. Maroussia had been granted permission to return to the Soviet Union. I thanked him and went straight to Breslav's. "Now," he admitted, "you are really in a spot. If you refuse to go, you lose your job and will be expelled from the union." I didn't care, I told him, and I reminded him that even though he had left Russia before World War I, he didn't want to go back. How much more so in my case. I had fought the Soviets for two years, my whole family had served in the White Army, and everybody was dead. No matter how you sliced it, the whole deal was unacceptable. I was not a Soviet citizen, I had not requested citizenship. How dare they simply order me to return? "You will have to so inform the consul," I concluded.

When Breslav returned, he told me that the consulate was in an uproar and the consul himself wanted to see me. I agreed on the condition that we meet in Breslav's home. That night, over dinner, Breslav asked me why I was in such a state about going back to Russia. "But it's obvious," I told him. "I'm afraid." He seemed unwilling to just accept that. He asked me why I was afraid and told me I would be given a hero's reception. Even he did not seem to understand why, after having lived all these years on my own, I would be so resentful at being handed a fait accompli by a government I had no relation to, and every reason to resent and distrust. Furthermore, I assured him, after all these years, I was not sure I could find the treasure; it might have been discovered and taken away (I was pretty sure this could not be true, but I spoke with conviction). "How would the authorities react to that? I would be a traitor, an officer of Wrangel's army, an enemy of the people. It would mean Siberia."

The next day even Breslav advised me to refuse. If it had not been for the money I had gotten from the Americans, I would have been desperate, because I couldn't get a Belgian work permit. And now I had lost my job.

15

An End to My Prisons

SO I BEGAN TO THINK about the treasure again. I had to have a good deal of money to go after it again, and now I would have to obtain a new passport under a different name, since the Soviets knew all about me. I also needed at least two people to help me, and that too would cost money. I couldn't go to anyone for backing. They would want to know who I was, and if they breathed one word to the Belgian police, I would be arrested again as a swindler.

I had to make some money. Every morning Maroussia applied a yellow liquid to her hair. When I asked her what it was, she told me that her father, who was a doctor, had invented a way of restoring color to graying hair. After a number of experiments, I was finally persuaded that it did work. We planned to merchandise it, and I christened it Serebrine, from the Russian word for silver. At first, we were refused permission to manufacture and sell it in Belgium but after it was tested in government laboratories, we got a license. We set about the task of introducing it to the market with our extremely limited resources.

Our business went only moderately well. A bottle of Serebrine sold for a hundred and thirty Belgian francs, and though sales were good, we didn't gross enough to cover our costs. Advertising was very dear, and even though we sold only for cash, our expenses ate up seventy-two percent of what we took in. I had tried to raise capital from a number of sources, but some were skeptical about the product and others had imposed unacceptable conditions. It would be a pity to throw in the towel so soon. We had put up a lot of money and effort into it, and we had never had a single complaint from a customer. In fact, we had letters from all over the country testifying to the product's effectiveness. We had no outstanding debts on Serebrine, and if I had had a job, I could have liquidated the business, but I could not get a work permit, and if the Belgian police were to discover that I was unemployed, they would expel me from the country without a passport.

I was so worried I could not sleep nights. This was the time of the war between the People's Republic of China under Mao and Nationalist China under Chiang Kai-shek. My sympathies were with Mao, who seemed to be the weaker. The Americans were completely on Chiang's side and were pouring an enormous amount of aid into his campaign. He was using their money for luxuries. I decided to get hold of some of that money.

First of all, I studied everything I could find on what was going on in China. I received some Soviet journals that were not very widely circulated in the West. When I felt I knew enough to discuss the Chinese situation with anyone, I called up the Chinese ambassador in Brussels. I told him I had something important to communicate to his government and asked to see him as soon as possible. The next day I went to the embassy and was received by the ambassador, a man of infinite charm and refinement.

The plan I had devised to assist Mao — like the document on the Soviet meeting that I had furnished to the Americans — has never been found out as phony. I told him there was a Soviet headquarters organized to offer assistance to Mao, located in Kharbin, a Russian city in Manchuria. From the Soviet publications, I knew the names of the generals stationed in Siberia and who among them had contacts with Mao. Because I was able to include many of the real facts about the situation and the personnel in Manchuria, my story rang true. My connection with the Union of Soviet Patriots was also well known (only Breslav knew that I had been expelled) and I still went regularly to the restaurant run by the union. It was generally believed that I had been relieved of my duties in order to prepare for my departure to the Soviet Union, or because I had received a new assignment.

The Chinese ambassador was enthusiastic about my offer to pass him information about Russian aid to Mao. He cabled Marshal Chiang immediately, and a few days later he informed me that my offer had been accepted. He would pay me for any information I gave him on a scale running between two hundred thousand and five hundred thousand Belgian francs. I accepted. For the next three years I passed on all kinds of false information and was well paid for it.

But eventually the arrangement came to an end. One night the ambassador summoned me urgently. I was afraid I had been found out, but I could hardly refuse to go. We met in a supper club in the city and the ambassador was very nervous. Chiang had told him to obtain exact intelligence on the Red strategy for the inevitable battle at the Yellow River. I had never before been asked for such precise information; ordinarily, I furnished rather general information about Soviet assistance and various projects. I told him information would be hard to come by, that it would take at least two weeks, and that I could not guarantee anything. For the next two weeks I pored over all the news sources I could lay my hands on, and I stared at a map of China that I kept in my apartment. Then I prepared a report and presented it to the ambassador, pretending, as I always did, that I had got it from a Soviet diplomat in Brussels who had connections in Moscow. Once again, my so-called information turned out to be correct. Chiang's army was defeated and had to withdraw to Formosa. A week later, the ambassador called me again, but I decided to call this particular arrangement to a halt.

I furnished other such "interesting" information to a number of embassies, including the Mexicans. One day as I was leaving their embassy, carrying the cash I had just been paid for a "document," I was picked up by two policemen and taken to a nearby station house. They confiscated the money (though they gave me a receipt). The ambassador had his information now, and evidently he wanted his money back. However, since we both posted a claim on the money, neither of us could get it. Some time later, the Mexicans threatened to denounce me to the Soviets unless I withdrew and allowed them to recover their money. I did what they asked but they denounced me anyhow.

I was obliged to tell the whole story to the counselor of the Soviet embassy in Brussels. He scolded me for giving their counterintelligence service such a bad name. I explained that after the Union of Soviet Patriots had thrown me out I had no other way to make a living. He was understanding but had no advice to offer. He was very flattering about the "document" I had sold the Americans, although he said that any Soviet expert would have known it was false right off the bat from some of the language. "Anyhow, congratulations," he said. "It was a great job."

I don't want to name all the embassies to whom I sold information, but there were many. My career in this line of work came to an end, however, some time later in Switzerland. I had fallen ill in Vevay and couldn't pay my hotel bill and, as a result, I was not thinking clearly. I wrote the United States embassy in Berne offering them important information from the Soviet Union. But I neglected to keep my fingerprints off the letter and they checked them as a matter of course. When I telephoned the embassy to follow up, I was told to go to a café near the federal capitol. There, I would get a telephone call and be told the exact time and place for a conference. I was suspicious, but I had no choice. When I arrived, the café was empty except for two very engrossed couples and a lone man reading a newspaper. It looked too well-staged, but I sat down at a table and ordered a coffee. A few minutes later the telephone rang and the owner announced, "A call for Monsieur Nicholas." I waited a moment before I got up and said, "That's me." I hadn't taken three steps before all five of them had me surrounded.

The man who had been reading the newspaper was a Swiss federal police inspector named Muller. Very politely, he asked me to come along with him. I told the police that the Americans had cheated me of some money a few years back and that I was simply trying to get it back. They held me for about three weeks and then Muller, again very politely, invited me to leave Switzerland.

So I returned to Brussels, where the sales of my home-made secret documents had been providing me with the capital to finance the Serebrine enterprise. Business was better and I was looking forward to future prosperity. Unfortunately, just then I got myself into another tight spot. While I was still on good terms with the Soviets, I had undertaken a project for them in order to raise money for another expedition to Bulgaria. I had a franchise to import typewriters from East Germany — then the Soviet zone of occupation — and to sell them in Western Europe. I had to pay for shipping and insurance and had to borrow over a million Belgian francs from four different individuals; the business and financial arrangements were very complicated. I was late in repaying my creditors.

Two of them, to whom I owed altogether six hundred thousand francs, were getting impatient. To get them off my back, I paid them off, but I was still in debt to the tune of another six hundred thousand francs. I was looking for a way to raise the additional money.

To add to my troubles, the chief inspector of the Belgian security police had it in for me. Somehow he learned that I owed P. two hundred thousand francs, his investment in the German typewriter deal plus interest. Once he found out, he persuaded P. that I had to be deported as a security risk.

P. visited me. "Listen," he said, "this typewriter business is dragging on too long. The money I loaned you isn't mine. It belongs to my uncle and he is getting very nervous."

"What can I do? Why not bring him here and I'll explain things to him."

"That's okay but he won't believe you unless you show him something in writing. You must have something official in writing."

"Nothing but the original letter from Berlin that you read."

"So what? Make something up. We'll show it to him and tear it up afterward."

"Okay, bring him around to your house tomorrow. But I must have your word of honor that I can tear up the paper as soon as he leaves."

I went to the consulate and typed some notes about shipping and other details on Soviet letterhead. The next day P. introduced me to his "uncle." We had a drink and chatted about this and that. Then I brought up business. I assured him that everything was going well but that if he wanted to withdraw his investment, I would repay him the following week. As I said this, I took out the letter and handed it to him. He read it carefully and then folded it and calmly put it in his pocket. "What are you doing?" I said. "Why are you taking my letter?"

"Because it is a forgery and I am placing you under arrest," he said, pulling out his police badge. I was convicted and put in prison.

Needless to say, the Serebrine company foundered. Maroussia could not keep it going alone, and when I was released, I was issued a travel permit and ordered to leave Belgium. It was clear that I would never obtain the legal right to settle anywhere with such a document. My only choices were to get a passport of some kind or give up, and I was not ready to give up. I bought myself a good passport and with it I operated in several European countries as a clandestine export-import liaison between Western and Eastern Europe. Naturally, this was entirely extralegal, and I was often assumed to be a Russian spy. At one point, an official of the Ministry of the Interior refused to issue me a permit to settle in France because I had not paid any taxes. But how could I pay taxes when my official identity was false?

For four months I did manage to live legally in Paris but it meant going to the police headquarters constantly to get my permit renewed, and the official from the Ministry of the Interior hounded me incessantly. Finally, I was assigned to live in Rennes, in Brittany. Rennes is a charming city, but I looked everywhere for a job, and after two months I had to face up to the fact that there was nothing there I could do. I had to get someplace else. To lead the kind of clandestine life I did, you have to have at least three passports. It's very tricky. I was arrested once in Nice for using a false name and not having a residence permit and sent to prison in Aix-en-Provence. Because I was a middle-aged man, I was assigned to the infirmary and there I made a new and extraordinary acquaintance. For whatever reason, a man presented himself at the prison one fine day and simply said, "I am Paul Leca. I want to give myself up." I had been immediately impressed with the deference with which both guards and prisoners treated him. It turned out that Paul Leca was a famous gangster, who had been involved in a theft of some of Begum Aga Khan's jewels. He had subsequently disappeared in South America for a while. His return was signaled by a series of gangland murders in Corsica and southern France. Various inconvenient witnesses were being eliminated one by one. He was a fascinating person and we spent a lot of time chatting about his adventures. Unfortunately, I did not have the chance to get to know him better. The court of appeals upheld my sentence and I was transferred to Les Baumettes to finish out my term. I brought a case of sausages from Leca to some of his friends there, and because I was known as a friend of his, I was once again put in the infirmary, a relatively comfortable spot.

Two years after that, I received a letter from Leca. He was out of prison and wanted to get together. He invited me to come to Nice, in the south of France, where he owned a restaurant. I was vacationing in Alassio in Italy and I wrote him that I preferred to meet there, since I was trying to steer clear of places where the police were likely to be on the lookout. He arrived after a few days and we had a splendid reunion. Leca made me several propositions, any of which would have bought me all the residence and work permits I could use, if I had simply accepted and then gone to the police. But I assured him I would do no such thing, thanked him for his friendship, and declined.

About this time I got interested in the *tierce*, which is a form of racetrack gambling very popular in France. I had come to the conclusion that it is possible to win quite a bit of money if one played the *tierce* systematically. Of course, it is necessary to place substantial bets. I figured out a system that has worked out quite well over the years, and I managed to win between sixty and one hundred thousand francs a year. But it is hard work. So that's the way I lived, betting and moving around. But I also met the last woman in my life. We have been together for almost eleven years and, even in the hardest times, she has never let me down.

16

Back to the Treasure

I DIDN'T THINK MUCH about the treasure then for a long time. But every so often the thought would come to me that if I died it would be gone forever. I finally decided that I had to do something about it, even if I couldn't find anybody to help. I finally wrote to the Bulgarian ambassador in Paris, telling him what was involved and offering to share what was left with the Bulgarian Government. He wrote back to say that he had forwarded my letter to Sofia. When I telephoned the ambassador a month later, he asked me to come to the embassy. I preferred to meet at a café nearby. He indicated that his government was inclined to accept, but wanted to know my conditions. I told him I would offer a proposal shortly.

My plan involved a friend in Paris who was a former member of the National Assembly. I approached him with it. The two of us would go to Bulgaria together, posing as simple tourists, during which time I would show him the first hiding place. At our ages, it would be physically impossible for us to actually dig it up. When we were back in Paris, I would inform the Bulgarians that my friend could conduct them to the first hiding place, but that he did not know any of the others. Whatever they recovered was to be transported to the French consulate, where it would be appraised by a Parisian expert whom I would send. My half of the treasure would be given to my friend to give to me.

The Frenchman and I agreed, but when I laid it out to the Bulgarians, I saw at a glance that it was unworkable. It was clear to me that they would immediately alert the Russians, who would claim the treasure as their rightful property. The plan had been impractical, but at least I was sure that the treasure was not in any immediate danger. Before I did anything more about it, however, I decided that I ought to go to Bulgaria to make sure that the hiding places were still intact. But it was a long time before I was able to make the voyage, only a few years ago. And that trip was a series of adventures.

I thought I might try to enter Bulgaria from Greece, where I had a friend who had been a fellow officer during the Civil War. Somehow, I had never been able to accept his invitations to visit him and his Greek wife. Now I went there to see them to tell him my plan. He said I had come to the right man. He could help. All I needed was a small solid boat and a reliable crew. He knew a captain who smuggled, but who was a man of his word and a good sailor. He arranged for us to meet. We went down into the old section of the city near the port and were admitted into a whitewashed stone building by an old woman. The captain was there, a giant of a man with a magnificent black beard and incredibly large hands and arms. My friend explained: I had to land in Bulgaria, stay there for about three days, and then go to an Italian port. The captain agreed to take me, and set a reasonable price. I was to take a regular ferry to the island where he kept his boat.

I had no trouble finding his boat in the little port. It looked like an ordinary fishing boat, with a sail and a motor, about twenty yards long. The captain was in the interior of the island on business. While I waited for him, I stayed at his house, which was luxurious and exquisitely furnished with Oriental rugs. He threw a party for me the evening he returned, with members of his crew and a small orchestra. Greek wine and the local cognac flowed like water and a whole lamb was cooked on a grill.

Two days later we set out. I had paid for my trip in dollars and the captain had said that he was going to purchase Bulgarian tobacco while we were there. He promised me that he would not sell it illegally until after he had landed me at an Italian port. We left the island about 4 P.M. As we came close to the entrance to the Dardanelles toward evening, the captain told me that a storm was brewing and that he would have to put in at a small port on one of the islands. We didn't make it, however. The waves grew huge and the wind howled. The boat pitched so deeply that I thought it would turn over. I was certain we would sink. I lay on my bed, since I could not stand without cracking my head against the walls of my cabin. The storm raged until 3 A.M. and then began to calm down. About 5 A.M., as dawn was breaking, I looked outside the cabin. I could hear the captain's voice just outside my door. When I opened it, there he was, and I have never been so happy to see anyone in my life. He smiled at me through his magnificent beard. "So, you are still alive."

He had not been able to reach any of the islands, of course. And, in fact, for the moment we had had to stay as far from land as possible so as not to be driven onto the beach. There was some damage to the boat but nothing serious. It could be repaired in a few days and then we would continue on our way. Eventually, we stopped at a small village on one of the islands, where I spent a very pleasant two days. Then we went to Constantinople, where we purchased fuel and provisions. The next day we pushed on and soon we had entered the Black Sea, which I have always been in love with.

But before we got to Bulgaria, the captain came to my cabin. "I don't know why you are going to Bulgaria," he said, "and I don't care. All I ask is that you do nothing to cause trouble between me and these people. As far as I'm concerned, you are a tourist on a pleasure cruise. And you know nothing about my business. Right?" I assured him that he had nothing to worry about. "I have come to check on some personal business," I said. "That's all." It was the truth.

Before I even thought seriously about trying to recover the treasure, I had to make sure it was still there. I had no doubts that it was, but I wanted to find out whether the terrain had altered. Perhaps the woods had been cut down, or somebody might have built on the site. We landed, and after the usual formalities, the captain headed for Plovdiv, the center of the tobacco market. He gave me three days' leave before I had to be back at the boat.

Disembarking was easy. The customs officials were very friendly. The city had changed tremendously since I had been there last and I did not recognize many of the streets. I strolled around all that day, and set out on my expedition toward evening. I was wearing old clothes so as to melt easily into the general population.

By daybreak I had reached the first hiding place. It was undisturbed. By late afternoon I had found the other three spots. They too were untouched. All this had taken longer than I had planned and I was physically exhausted as well. Since I couldn't leave until it was completely dark, I stretched out to catch a nap. I must have been asleep for about three hours when I was awakened by voices nearby. Two men were talking and were evidently awaiting a third person. They may have been bandits. In any case, I was afraid to move even an inch because the noise of the dry leaves would have given me away.

I drew my pistol slowly. My back and legs were aching. I didn't know whether they were armed. This went on for about two hours, and then I heard a dog barking. The Bulgarians called out. It must have been their friend with his dog. The damn dog would certainly discover me. In a few minutes, the dog had picked up my scent. He began to bark and growl. At first the men must have thought he had found some animal. He was right on top of me and I was sure he was about to go for my throat, when I shot him in the snout, leaped up with my gun drawn, and ordered them to hold their hands up. I had taken them completely by surprise. To my relief I could see they were not armed, though each carried a big club. I told them to throw their clubs down. They realized immediately from my accent that I was Russian. All to the good. It made them all the more careful. I asked them what they were doing there. They told me some cock-and-bull story about looking for a lost dog. I said that was nonsense and that they could be shot as thieves. "Get out of here, fast," I said, and they set out running.

By about 5 A.M. I was almost back at the port. I lay down in a small woods nearby for about an hour and then went back on board. Once back in my cabin, I slept for fourteen hours, almost till midnight. I had some supper and spent the rest of the night reading. Early the next morning, I heard the captain come back aboard and went out to greet him. "We will leave tomorrow," he said. "I haven't been able to do any business but I hope your affairs went well."

As we entered the Aegean the captain asked whether it was all right with me if we changed course. "It will add two or three days to the trip," he said, "but you will see islands most tourists have never seen." I had nothing better to do and it seemed like a delightful prospect. That night I went to sleep peacefully.

About 1 A.M. I was awakened by shouting and screaming on the deck. I could hear people running around and falling down. I ran up to see what was going on. I couldn't believe my eyes. There were about twenty men attacking our crew. The captain was fighting like a madman, with his back up against the mast. I saw him pick a man up and heave him into the sea. Then someone hit me over the head.

When I came to, I had a fierce pain in the back of my neck and I couldn't move. My hands were tied behind my back and there were irons on my ankles. And I was thirsty as the very devil, my mouth so dry I couldn't even call out. I had a fantasy that I had fallen into the hands of men who knew about the treasure and were going to torture me to find out the secret.

I was in a dark room and on land. I couldn't hear a sound, and I could barely make out my surroundings. Then I lost consciousness again. When I awoke the next time I was astonished to find myself in a well-lighted room, lying on a clean bed. Just as I was getting ready to call for help and ask for something to drink, a young man came into the room with two pitchers, one of cold water and the other of white wine. He spoke to me in Greek, which I could not understand. Nor could he comprehend any of the languages I tried out on him. Then he began to count with his fingers. When he saw that I still did not understand, he lowered the lamp and raised it again, holding up seven fingers. I understood that he was telling me that I would have to wait until seven o'clock. He was not wearing a watch but when I pointed to his wrist, he held up his fingers to indicate that it was 11 A.M. I pointed to the wound on my head and groaned. He left and came back after a few minutes with an old, toothless crone dressed all in black. When she saw my wound, she began to scold the young man. Then they both left. I thought I wouldn't see them again.

After a half hour they returned. She was carrying a bowl of hot water and a big wad of absorbent cotton. He had some cold meat, goat cheese, and bread and fruit. The woman gestured for me to turn over. Then she washed my wound with water and bathed it with an evil-smelling liquid which, to my surprise, eased the pain. Then she set a plate full of food in front of me. They both wished me *kalispera*, "good night," and left.

My appetite had come back and I ate heartily. I was still trying to understand what in the world was going on. At last, even in my state, I dismissed the idea that it had anything to do with the treasure. The only person in Greece who knew anything about it was my Russian friend, whom I trusted absolutely. I decided to put it out of my mind and try to get some sleep.

When I woke up the next morning, two men were standing over me, staring at me with curiosity but with no apparent hostility. "Good morning," one of them said in fairly good French. "How did you sleep?"

"How could I sleep well when here I am kidnapped and tied without knowing why? What's going on?"

The one who spoke French translated for his companion, who was clearly his superior. They were both well dressed in European style. The more important man wore an expensive suit and a gold watch. He wanted to know who I was, what I had been doing on the boat, and how long and how well I knew the captain. I asked if they were from the police and they answered, "We are as far from the police as the moon is from the earth."

They were gangsters. The captain and I had agreed on what my story should be if anyone wanted to know what I was doing on board his boat. So I told them that I was a former officer of the Russian White Army and that therefore I couldn't safely enter any communist countries. But I had had my heart set on going to Bulgaria to see my only sister, who had married a Bulgarian. This seemed to satisfy them. I hoped the captain had stuck to our story.

They wanted to know if I knew why the captain went back and forth to Bulgaria. I said I didn't and that if they knew the captain, they also knew that he was not the kind of man one questioned too closely. Without another word they turned to leave, and the interpreter said, "Monsieur is satisfied with your answers. You will learn his decision this evening."

I looked out through the barred window. The building was about two hundred yards from the sea and in the distance I could see a tiny island. I was almost certainly on one of those tiny islands in the Sporades and therefore far from any of the main routes. The time passed slowly as I waited to learn what "Monsieur" had decided. It was quite late when the interpreter finally returned. He handed me an envelope.

"Monsieur regrets," he said, "that you have been so badly treated. Here is a thousand dollars. He wants you to accept it to make up for the unjust treatment you have received. Tomorrow, a doctor will come to take care of you. In the meanwhile, the old woman who took care of you last night will look after you. In a couple of days you can leave here with the captain, provided he agrees to make retribution for the harm he has done us. If he refuses, we will take you to any port that you choose. There is only one condition: you must swear to tell no one what has happened. It is to your advantage to accept this condition, because the police are after both the captain and us and I promise you they will give you nothing but trouble if they find out about all this."

I swore I would speak to no one. Immediately afterward, the old woman and the young man came with fresh bandages and food. They also had a large jug of cool white wine. The old lady was so gentle with me that after she had cleaned my wound, I kissed her on both cheeks. She placed her hand softly on my head and said something that I would have given anything to understand. When they left, I ate, then drank the whole jug of wine and threw myself on the bed quite drunk. The next morning the young man woke me and escorted me to another building. It had the same plain exterior but was very luxurious inside. He took me to a bathroom, where I was overjoyed to find my baggage, my papers and my books. I shaved, bathed, and changed my clothes.

When I came out, he was waiting for me. "In a few days," he said, "you will be far from here, and I believe your friend the captain will be the one to take you. He is being quite reasonable and there is peace between us now." I was delighted. He led me into a drawing room, beautifully furnished in the Middle Eastern style, and offered me some strong Turkish coffee. Just then a small man, also dressed in the European style, appeared in the doorway and announced in perfect German that he was a doctor. He examined my wound and pronounced it not serious. The swelling was already going down. He rebandaged it, and advised me to keep it covered for three days and after that to let nature take its course.

These gangsters were treating me so graciously that I was beginning to feel at home. I was almost ready to forgive them for my injury and the brutal way they had treated me. It must be a matter of two rival gangs involved in the same illicit traffic. All I hoped was that my part in their adventures would soon be over.

I saw the captain again about noon. The door opened suddenly and there he was — covered with bruises and almost his entire head in bandages. He threw his arms around me and kissed me on both cheeks. "My friend," he said, "I am so glad to see you. I hope you are feeling better. Forgive me for this frightful experience. I had no idea. One day they will pay for it. Someone — it had to be someone in my crew — betrayed me. I'll find out who it was and then he had better watch out."

The young man came to lead us to another room, where we were served an excellent lunch. The captain told me that he had lost two men. The cook had been killed and a sailor had been fatally wounded. The attackers had also had two killed, both by the captain himself. The boat had suffered some damage but would be able to embark in a couple of days. I thought it best not to ask what had been the cause of the trouble. Once before, I had asked him what I had imagined was a harmless question and he had changed from a friendly companion into a cold, terrifying stranger.

That evening, the chief, who was leaving the next day, gave a banquet to celebrate his reconciliation with the captain. We ate bounteously and drank gallons of wine until four o'clock in the morning. Everybody got drunk, including me. The men drew their pistols and started firing into the ceiling. At the end the chief brought two pretty dancers who had entertained during the evening to the captain and me. Unfortunately, I was so drunk that I fell asleep as soon as I hit the bed.

That afternoon the captain and I walked around the island. I tried to find out where we might be by referring to Lemnos. He pretended not to understand. Honor among thieves. He would not betray his own enemies.

The next day, the captain was as anxious as I to leave. Since there was no wind, he started up the engine, and soon we were far from the island. The two missing crew members had somehow been replaced. The captain was in a bad mood, and I understood he was brooding about the traitor who had given away his course and the enormous sum he must have had to pay to ransom himself, his crew and his boat.

He got his revenge on the traitor that night. After dinner we were playing checkers when he announced suddenly that he was going to retire. I was exhausted and only too willing. I fell asleep immediately, and was awakened by such terrible and bloodcurdling screams that I covered my ears. I was sure the captain was extracting a confession from the suspect.

The next morning he asked me if I had slept well. I answered, "Never better." But about noon I noticed that the old helmsman was missing. The captain himself was at the rudder. Three days later he let me off at the same port from which I had embarked, and before I left he gave me back the money I had paid him. "You were almost killed and it was all my fault," he said. "Take this money and don't give me any argument. Just keep all this to yourself."

When I saw my old Russian friend again, I had to tell him all about my trip. He was terribly upset that he had put me in such danger. "Not at all," I told him. "I had to see if it was still there."

I spent a week with him and his wife, and though they wanted me to stay longer I decided I had to get away from Greece. I wanted to go home. All that was left for me now was to dream about the treasure of the White Army buried in an obscure Bulgarian forest.

Only I know where.